THE **18**
LAWS OF
LEVERAGE

The Ultimate Blueprint for
Exponential Wealth

THE **18** LAWS OF LEVERAGE

NATE HAMBRICK

ISBN Paperback: 979-8-9857010-4-3
ISBN Hardcover: 979-8-9857010-5-0
ISBN Audiobook: 979-8-9857010-6-7
ISBN ebook: 979-8-9857010-7-4

CLAIM YOUR
FREE AUDIOBOOK!

As a thank you for buying *The 18 Laws of Leverage*, I want to give you the audiobook version—completely free!

Research shows that listening while reading improves comprehension and helps us finish books faster, so I'm giving you the audio version to maximize the results you get from this book. Enjoy!

18LAWSAUDIO.NATEHAMBRICK.COM

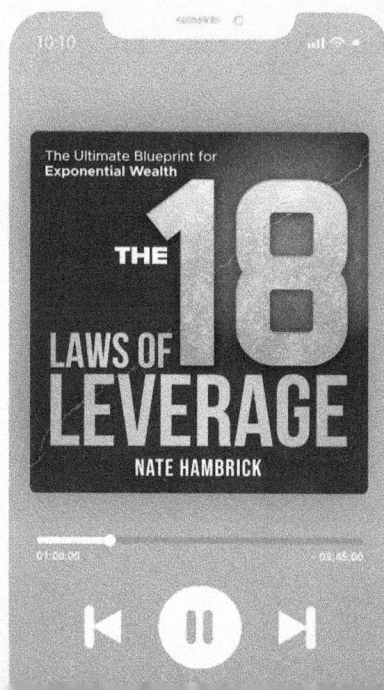

Dedication

To my father, a man of quiet strength and profound wisdom. He taught me through his words and actions that the best way to help people is to become the best version of yourself so you can teach the willing and help those who cannot help themselves.

"Give me a lever long enough and a fulcrum on which to place it, and I shall move the world."

—Archimedes

CONTENTS

CONTENTS

Introduction

Life has a way of unraveling when you least expect it. My world began to fall apart on a Monday afternoon in the fall of 2020.

Just as I was getting a handle on the chaotic workweek, my office door creaked open, and my wife walked in.

"I just got laid off," she told me in a hushed tone.

This was the third round of layoffs due to the pandemic and a series of disastrous decisions made by upper management. I rose from my chair and comforted her, summoning every ounce of confidence I could muster.

Like almost everyone else, our pandemic years were riddled with emotional, physical, mental, and financial stress. Our car was in the shop with unknown repair costs. We were planning to move, and expenses were piling up. I was stuck in an insurance job I hated, and now everything seemed even more uncertain. The world felt like it was closing in on all sides, crushing us with mounting bills and unexpected expenses. We were caught in the perfect storm.

Sitting at the kitchen table that night, surrounded by the remains of a hastily prepared dinner, it hit me. "Remember that real estate investment we made a few years ago? Hasn't that been paying us a thousand bucks a month for a while now?"

At the time, $1K a month didn't seem like much, so we set it up to be automatically deposited into a bank account that we rarely checked. However, over time, it accumulated into a nest egg worth $20K.

We didn't realize its impact until we needed it, but that small $1K drip of passive income became our lifeline in the storm, proving that even a little bit of leverage can have a profound effect. Our initial fear transformed into excitement about the future. We had always dreamed of escaping the nine-to-five grind, and now we had the opportunity to create the life we wanted.

"Forget the job search," I said. "What if we turned a thousand into ten thousand a month? What if we multiplied that by a hundred?" That was our moment to reimagine and reinvent the way we lived.

That modest little nest egg showed me that leverage can make a big impact. At that moment, I knew I wanted more! What I didn't know (at that time) was that I'd only discovered one of the many forms of leverage, and there were so many new forms yet to be discovered.

Three years later, we were living the dream. We had multiplied our efforts and were now generating a steady stream of passive income from a variety of sources. Today, we receive monthly payments from twelve corporations and over 300 individuals through rental checks, royalty checks, and other income streams. We've also multiplied our active income by five times and our passive income infinitely, creating a better life for our family.

Our previous reality is hardly unique. In today's world, working harder isn't enough to create wealth. There just aren't enough hours in the day to become a billionaire through hard work alone.

So how do we increase the results we get from our efforts?

The key is *leverage*.

Most people never get rich because they don't understand leverage. The ancient Greek mathematician Archimedes once said, "Give me a lever long enough and a fulcrum on which to place it, and I shall move the world."

That's leverage.

Leverage is anything that acts as a multiplier between the input and effort you give and the output and result you get. When used correctly, leverage offers disproportionate advantages and produces exponential results.

While hard work is essential, the most successful people understand that their true power lies in leveraging the assets at their disposal.

Walmart leverages labor with over 2.3 million employees.[1] Berkshire Hathaway leverages capital to multiply their returns. MrBeast and Kylie Jenner leverage media to monetize attention. Uber leverages code to facilitate billions of transactions. It's not just about working hard—it's about the mechanisms deployed to create continuous wealth. That's why some people only make money when they work, while others make money in their sleep.

I've succeeded in building wealth through leverage, but I'm an outlier. I wish I weren't. I want my experience to be the norm. I want everyone to be wealthy—and that's the goal of this book. Through these eighteen laws, I will show you how to build wealth the way billionaires do, on as small or as large a scale as you want.

Welcome to *The 18 Laws of Leverage: The Ultimate Blueprint for Exponential Wealth*. This is a behind-the-scenes look at the principles that have propelled the world's most successful individuals to extraordinary heights. From industry leaders and tech innovators to celebrity artists and athletes, these laws are the driving force behind their meteoric rise.

The insights in this book will transform the way you earn, produce, and leave a legacy. Each law is illustrated with real-world examples, practical advice, and actionable steps.

This book will teach you how to:

- **Leverage the capital and skill sets of others** to multiply your output. (Laws Two through Four)

- **Monetize your reputation** through partnerships, sponsorships, and endorsements. (Law Five)

- **Buy your victories** instead of working for them. (Law Six)

- **Turn liabilities you already own into assets** that pay you monthly. (Law Thirteen)

- **Create scalable products** once that can be sold infinitely. (Law Fourteen)

- **Acquire assets** that produce income independently of your day-to-day efforts. (Law Sixteen)

- **Leverage accelerated depreciation** to lower your taxable income so you keep more of your earnings. (Law Seventeen)

- **Harness the attention economy.** (Law Eighteen)

By the end of this book, you'll have a war chest of wealth-creation strategies ready to deploy.

Imagine a world where your every action generates exponential results, your efforts are magnified, and your goals are finally within reach.

All you must do is master the art of leverage.

A Warning Against Waiting

Don't fall into the trap of thinking you have time to spare. Every day you delay is a day you could be compounding your wealth and securing your financial future. There will never be a perfect time to take control of your financial destiny—so start now. Open this book, embrace the power of leverage, and watch your world transform.

Welcome to the world of leverage. I wish you all the luck on your journey to success—but once you read this book, you won't need luck at all.

THE 18 LAWS OF LEVERAGE

Stand on the Shoulders of Giants

"He who can read and write has four eyes."

—Albanian Proverb

In the fall of 1980, Mark, an ambitious junior at Indiana University, began his entrepreneurial journey.[2] His first venture was purchasing a struggling bar called The Silver Dollar. Despite barely being of legal drinking age himself, Mark saw potential in the location and believed that with the right strategy, it could regain its popularity. Recognizing the need for a fresh start, Mark renamed the bar Motley's Pub and set out to make it a success.

It wasn't easy, but with his vision, Motley's Pub transformed into a popular destination for college students seeking lively parties. Mark knew how to draw a crowd and keep them coming back. He was thriving. After all his hard work, things were beginning to fall into place. For a brief moment, it seemed like Motley's Pub would be his ticket to a successful life.

Unfortunately, a few months later, Mark's instant success came to an abrupt halt when law enforcement shut down the pub for serving alcohol to minors. It was an oversight on Mark's part; in the excitement of the pub's rapid success, he had neglected to follow regulations.

Like the best entrepreneurs, Mark was undeterred by this setback. He knew he was onto something and was determined to develop his business skills. So he turned to books for the knowledge he needed to build a successful business. He became an avid reader, devoting every minute of free time to devouring books on business, technology, economics, sales, marketing, and leadership. He spent his days and nights educating himself on the nuances of the business world and learning how to make better, more calculated decisions moving forward.

One of the first books Mark read was *The Art of War* by Sun Tzu, which taught him the importance of strategy and planning. *Think and Grow Rich* by Napoleon Hill showed him the power of positive thinking and the importance of setting actionable goals. And the biographies of entrepreneurs such as Andrew Carnegie and John Rockefeller taught Mark the value of hard work, perseverance, and the power of innovation.

As he read, Mark noticed patterns in the stories of successful entrepreneurs. They all shared a few common traits: their work ethic, willingness to take risks, and strategies were all fueled by a relentless determination to succeed. Even in the face of insurmountable odds, they always found ways to push forward.

Although they shared many similar traits, the most common trend among them was that they all had role models who guided their decisions. Their relentless pursuit of knowledge through reading allowed them to continuously evolve, adapt, and avoid costly mistakes.

Mark knew that if he wanted to join the ranks of these entrepreneurs, he had to adopt their mindsets and approaches and *stand on the shoulders of giants*. As he read, he absorbed their experience and wisdom and applied it to his ventures. He took their strategies, adopted their mindsets, and preemptively avoided their mistakes. It wasn't easy, but like the giants before him, Mark refused to let anything stand in his way.

The road to success was far from smooth for Mark. After graduating, he tried various jobs like most people his age, but they lasted only a short time. He was fired from or quit his first three jobs in a row. It wasn't a lack of work ethic—Mark thrived on challenges and hard work. The problem was that these jobs either didn't challenge him enough or didn't align with his goals.

Mark found a better path based on the knowledge he gained from books. The lessons from *The Art of War* and *Think and Grow Rich* had instilled in him the importance of strategy, planning, and positive thinking. Inspired by the success stories of Carnegie and Rockefeller, Mark was determined to create something that truly matched his skills and ambitions. This led him to start his own company, MicroSolutions.

MicroSolutions was a perfect fit for Mark's talents and interests. He applied the strategic insights of Sun Tzu to outmaneuver the competition and the principles of Napoleon Hill to set clear, actionable goals. He learned from his past experiences and the wisdom of his mentors to build an innovative and resilient company. His relentless reading had equipped him with the knowledge to navigate the complex world of technology and business.

Mark's dedication paid off when MicroSolutions was acquired for $6 million. But he didn't stop there. Armed with the lessons from his reading and experience, he built another company, Broadcast.com, and rode the booming Internet wave. This was later acquired by Yahoo! for $5.7 billion.[3] Mark even bought the lion's share of his favorite basketball team for $285 million and has continued to build and invest in many other companies.

At this point in our story, you probably recognize the man. This is the story of Mark Cuban, former owner of the Dallas Mavericks and one of the stars of *Shark Tank*. Forbes currently estimates his net worth is over $4.2 billion.

Oh, and Mark *still* reads more than three hours every day.

Replicating Greatness

Mark Cuban's success is a testament to the power of standing on the shoulders of giants. Through self-education, he gained the wisdom that would help him achieve his wildest entrepreneurial dreams.

When it comes to learning from business giants through books, he's hardly alone. Countless TV stars, politicians, and CEOs cite their reading habits as the source of their success. Actress Emilia Clarke says she's learned to "never trust anyone whose TV is bigger than their bookshelf."

Rick Warren, an influential Christian leader, reads one book a day and has 35,000 books in his home library.[4] Phil Knight, the founder of Nike, respects his books so much that he requires guests to remove their shoes when entering his library. Another billionaire entrepreneur,

David Rubenstein, reads six books a week. Most CEOs of Fortune 500 companies read an average of four to five books a month—that's about one book a week.[5] Mark Zuckerberg reads a book every two weeks. Oprah also attributes a lot of her success to reading.

"I just sit in my office and read all day," Warren Buffett said when asked how he became so successful.[6] He makes it sound so simple—sit and read. He reads five to six hours a day; his quota is five newspapers and 500 pages of reports.

Warren Buffett's right-hand man, Charlie Munger, is not much different. "As long as I have a book in my hand, I don't feel like I'm wasting time," said Charlie.[7]

Modern celebrities aren't the only ones who have this mindset either. Abraham Lincoln might have had only one year of formal education, but he credited his success to his voracious appetite for reading. Thomas Jefferson owned one of the most comprehensive book collections of his time, which he later donated to the United States Congress, forming the foundation of the Library of Congress. It is said that Teddy Roosevelt, who came after him, read two books a day.

This fact is clear: People who have reached the top read a lot, regardless of their background, location, specialty, formal education, personality, or vision.

Some of the most impactful decisions I've made were based on concepts I learned from books. But let me be clear: Not all reading is *standing on the shoulders of giants*. I'm not encouraging you to race through books just to meet your reading goals. While it's important to read a lot, it's also important to read *the right way*. Many leaders call their reading habit *deliberate learning*. They *read*, then *reflect* on what they've read, brainstorm new ideas, and *apply* those concepts to their daily lives. Whether you read one book a month or seven, reading should not be a passive activity. It's meant to absorb knowledge that you can immediately apply to your life.

The way I see it, reading is one of the greatest cheat codes available because the most successful people in every field have already done the hard work for you. They've already made the worst mistakes. They've already faced the obstacles you're facing and they've found the solutions. Best of all, they've recorded, documented, condensed, and articulated all of their best insights for you in coherent and digestible packages.

Simon Sinek, author of *Start with Why* and *The Infinite Game*, documented his best insights on leadership, motivation, and creating positive organizational cultures. Brené Brown, author of *Daring Greatly* and *Atlas of the Heart*, shares her discoveries on how vulnerability and human connection can transform our personal and professional lives. Perry Marshall, author of *80/20 Sales and Marketing*, distills decades of invaluable marketing experience into practical strategies that increase ad conversions and enable companies to help more people. Millions more have recorded their expertise in easy-to-access books that you can start learning from in a matter of minutes.

Think about it: With all the answers at your fingertips, why would you reinvent the wheel?

Why waste days, weeks, years, or decades of your life solving problems that already have documented solutions? Why create something from scratch when you can replicate someone else's success?

Simple.

Don't. Instead, read.

Standing on the shoulders of giants gives us a massive competitive edge, but many people fail to leverage this valuable resource. Countless successful men and women have repeatedly stated that their achievements stem from the volume of books they read, and yet, *most* people read very little. One source cites that the average American reads just twelve books a year, and another says that half the population reads fewer than four books a year.[8] While the statistics vary from survey to survey, the fact remains that we generally read far less than we should. On top of that, a significant portion of what we do read doesn't improve our lives and is merely fluff to fill our time.

Reading books, attending seminars, and seeking mentorship is typically at the bottom of our priority lists, not the top. We prolong our mediocrity by believing we can do it *alone.* Ignoring the wisdom of other successful entrepreneurs won't make us more independent or successful; it will only limit our growth and stunt our progress.

The fastest and most efficient way to succeed is to learn from those who have already achieved what you want. If you refuse to follow the path that's already been laid out for you, take a step back and ask yourself why. Maybe it's because you don't know where to start. Maybe it's easier to give up on your dreams than to fight for them. Maybe the busyness of life has made it difficult to prioritize tasks that will lead to meaningful progress.

Whatever the reason, it's time to try the well-worn path and follow in the footsteps of the greats who came before you.

How many self-help books have you read in the last year? Whatever the number, can you do better? How many do you plan to read this year? With any luck, that number has already begun to increase—in fact, it already has! You're reading *this* book right now.

I encourage you to aggressively acquire the knowledge you need to win. Stop wasting time and energy reinventing the wheel and learn how to *stand on the shoulders of giants.*

The Power of Targeted Learning

There are more books, blogs, and YouTube training videos than you could consume in a hundred lifetimes. To maximize the tangible value you get from reading, it's important to be intentional about what you read. Our time for self-development is limited, so shifting our approach from random reading to targeted learning is critical.

Proactive reading should be focused on finding solutions to real-world problems. The books you read must improve your skills and get you where you want to go. That's why it's important to start with your end goal in mind. Make sure you choose the right books, blogs, and training videos to get you where you want to go; not everything is right for the task at hand. If you read with a clear goal in mind, you will make a lot more progress with the time you invest.

I used to blindly read popular self-help books without stopping to identify my biggest obstacles and then find the books that could solve them. Looking back, I realize that I wasted more time on business entertainment than on solving the roadblocks in my life.

Don't make the same mistake. It's important to make sure you're consistently finding ways to move forward on your ideal path, not settling for the path of least resistance. Make the most of your time. The books you read should solve urgent problems and immediately increase your production and, therefore, your income. The power of targeted learning lies in its ability to offer solutions, inspire change, and provide practical strategies to help you overcome obstacles and achieve your goals. Investing your time in reading things that transform your life must be a deliberate choice. It will never happen by accident. By aligning your reading material with your goals, you maximize the benefits that come from it.

If what you're reading still isn't producing tangible results, you may have one of two problems. Fortunately, they're both fairly easy to solve.

First, you may need to get off the reading couch and *apply* what you're learning. There comes a time when we have already absorbed everything our reading material has to offer the current version of ourselves. When that happens, it's important that you put the book down and start looking for practical applications for what you've already learned. As you do so, you will discover new obstacles—and that's when the cycle of learning can begin again.

The second problem is that you may simply be reading the wrong things and need to find new books to read. If you can't find tangible applications for the material you're reading, shift your focus to a new book topic.

Reading is one of the first keys to a better life. You just have to figure out what doors to open.

Permission to Quit

In a world that often equates quitting with failure, it's important to give yourself permission to stop reading books that aren't actively getting you results. Many of us have been conditioned from an early age to finish every book we start, whether it meets our needs or not. This obligation to complete unnecessary tasks overshadows the purpose of reading and sucks the fun out of it. Nothing makes learning more difficult than boredom. Reading is a personal investment in yourself and your well-being. If a book doesn't serve you, move on.

After all, time is one of your most precious resources. Reading books that offer little to no value is a poor investment. By focusing on relevant and inspiring material, you'll accelerate your growth and enjoy reading more, which should lead to finishing more books.

That's why the time-honored adage, "Focus on quality, not quantity," has stuck around for so long. While many would benefit from reading *more* books, the focus should be on the results you get from the books you read, not the quantity. So if you're feeling disengaged or struggling to maintain interest in the material, it's a sign that the book may not be right for you. Trust your instincts and move on to something more aligned with your interests and goals.

Giving yourself permission to quit a book is one of the fastest ways to increase your desire to read. You'll be surprised at how quickly your progress accelerates when you *stop* wasting time on unhelpful things.

The more you tap into the vast pool of wisdom and experience accumulated over centuries, the more you'll enjoy it and be amazed by the results.

Permission to Hire

Just as you give yourself permission to quit books that don't serve you, it's equally important to know when to seek help. As you learn new tactics and strategies, don't hesitate to hire an expert to handle tasks for you. You don't need to become an expert marketer, fitness trainer, capital raiser, and tax planner.

Success doesn't require mastery of every skill; it's about knowing which tasks are worth doing and ensuring they get done—whether by you or someone else.

There have been many times in my life where standing on the shoulders of giants has meant educating myself just enough to identify the next critical step and then hiring an expert to get me there. The depth of someone else's experience can move you forward much faster than struggling to achieve the same level of expertise on your own. This approach has allowed me to focus on my core strengths and passions while benefiting from the expertise of others.

As you learn new tactics, it's important to distinguish between those that align with your strengths and those better left to someone else. Master the skills that fall within your domain and delegate the rest. This strategy conserves your energy and accelerates your progress by allowing you to focus on what you do best. (We'll discuss this in more detail in the next chapter.)

By leveraging the expertise of others, you stand on the shoulders of giants in both understanding and execution. You tap into decades of knowledge and experience, bypassing the long, arduous process of trial and error. This advantage is invaluable because it saves you the most precious resources: time and energy.

So give yourself permission to let go of the need to do everything yourself. Embrace the support of experts, and watch your progress accelerate. Not only will your journey be more enjoyable, but you'll also reach your goals faster than you ever thought possible.

Reality Check:

Are you learning the easy way or the hard way?

If you're not currently standing on the shoulders of giants by reading their books, I encourage you to start. If you are but aren't getting tangible results, here are a few steps to increase your effectiveness and make it more enjoyable:

Define your goals: Identify the challenges in your work and find the books that will help you solve them.

Get recommendations: Ask your mentors for book recommendations, and be specific in your request. Ask for books that have given them the most results or books that solve specific challenges. Don't ask vague questions like, "What are your favorite books?"

Implement what you learn: The true value of reading comes from applying the knowledge to improve real-world situations. Challenge yourself to implement at least one idea from each book you read, and keep track of the tangible progress that comes from it.

Make it easy: Audiobooks and podcasts are great ways to stand on the shoulders of giants without having to make time to sit down and read. This is especially helpful for those who struggle to retain what they've learned through the written word. Audiobooks are the format I typically prefer; they have increased the quantity and quality of content I consume because I can learn while working out, driving, or performing other less productive and mundane tasks.

Choose books that align with your goals and transform the act of reading from a passive time waster to a dynamic tool for explosive growth.

Nate's Book Recommendations	Challenges They Solve
80/20 Sales and Marketing by Perry Marshall	Improve ad conversions and increase the results you get from your work.
From Passive to Passionate by Brian Luebben	Replace your income with passive income in three years or less so you're free to pursue your passions.
$100M Offers by Alex Hormozi	Boost your sales conversions by developing products that customers are more willing to pay for.
So Good They Can't Ignore You by Cal Newport	Learn how to become valuable to the marketplace and employers (great for those new to the workforce).
Growing Wealth in Self-Storage 2.0 by AJ Osborne	Learn how to create wealth in a less competitive asset class.
The Lifestyle Investor by Justin Donald	Create monthly income that is independent of your job or business.

Leveraged Action Steps

Acquiring knowledge is only half the journey; the real transformation happens when you apply these insights to your day-to-day life. Setting clear, actionable goals based on your reading will help you accomplish far more and ensure that the knowledge doesn't remain abstract but becomes a part of your lived experience.

At the end of each chapter, you'll find Leveraged Action Steps to help you implement the lesson and achieve tangible results. Here's an exercise to implement Law One immediately.

	Leveraged Action Steps	Your Notes
#1	**Identify Your Obstacles:** List the top three challenges you're currently facing.	
#2	**Find Resources:** Look for books that address each of your obstacles. Buy one book before you read the next chapter so that it's waiting for you when you finish reading this book.	
#3	**Find a Mentor:** Identify someone who is two to three steps ahead of you in life and can offer guidance. Make a list of potential mentors and contact one of them this week.	

Chapter One Takeaway

LAW ONE

Don't build anything from scratch.
Stand on the shoulders of giants by
leveraging the methods and strategies
of those who came before you

Use Other People's Money (OPM)

"No matter what you are purchasing, big or
small, always use other people's money."

—Professor Andrusco

Have you heard of real estate legends Grant Cardone and Robert
Kiyosaki? These icons built billion-dollar fortunes and have
demonstrated that to amass such wealth, you must leverage a critical
resource owned by others—money.

Grant Cardone is a master at using other people's capital to acquire
high-yield properties. Leveraging other people's money is a cornerstone
of his wealth-building strategy. Cardone's approach isn't just about
deploying his own capital; he knows he can accomplish far more by
putting other people's money to work for him. He excels at creating
win-win scenarios where all parties benefit. His deals are structured to
ensure that his investors receive a healthy return on their investment
while he exponentially grows his real estate empire with their capital.

Alongside Cardone stands Robert Kiyosaki, another real estate virtuoso and the acclaimed author of *Rich Dad, Poor Dad*. Kiyosaki has also built his vast wealth—with over 7,000 residential and commercial properties—through the strategic use of OPM.[2] Those who master the art of OPM can achieve financial freedom and enjoy an extraordinary, lavish lifestyle.

Many people misunderstand OPM and view it negatively, and I think part of the reason is that we often refer to OPM as debt, which has a negative connotation.

However, there is a crucial difference between credit card debt and leveraging capital to buy income-producing assets. The former will leave you broke, while the latter will make you rich.

Kiyosaki's financial strategy uses about $1.2 billion in OPM. If you call that number "debt," it's enough to make you weak in the knees. However, this is not personal debt; it's leveraged capital tied to income-producing assets. It's also important to note that the majority of this capital comes in the form of non-recourse loans—meaning that Kiyosaki is not personally liable if something goes wrong. This is a classic example of using other people's money to buy assets that pay for themselves and generate a profit.

OPM is a tool that needs to be fully understood before it can be applied, but fortunately the principle is simple. Imagine you've found an investment opportunity with great potential, but you need more capital to buy it. You borrow capital at a fixed cost, and as long as your investment earns more than the cost of the borrowed capital, you keep the difference. Finding investments with returns greater than the cost of borrowing is the cornerstone of leveraging capital well. The resulting *leveraged profit* is key to amassing wealth in any industry. And in real estate, most wealth is built by acquiring assets with OPM.

In a moment, I'll show you exactly how OPM works in other areas of wealth creation. But first, a quick disclaimer: While the strategies in this book are specific to the United States, many countries have similar applications. For now, let's focus more on the basics behind this law.

Seeking Leveraged Profit to Create Wealth

Most billionaires use *other people's money* more than they use their own. They do this because they understand that leveraging capital gives them incredible power. True wealth creators don't shy away from leveraging other people's resources. Instead, they use it to their advantage. It's an important lesson and a foundational step in understanding the laws of leverage.

OPM isn't just limited to real estate. It's applied in every facet of the business world. For instance, Warren Buffett launched his partnership using investor funds. Ray Kroc used franchising—that's another form of OPM—to expand McDonald's. Elon Musk uses a great deal of funding from investors and venture capitalists to build his organizations. Felix Dennis, one of Britain's richest self-made men, goes so far as to say, "If you want to become rich, you *need* to use other people's money."

He's right, and you can start implementing this form of leverage at any stage of life. That's the beauty of OPM. Take my friend Derek, for instance. He's a firefighter by trade. He financially retired after just twelve years in the workforce because he understood and properly applied the use of OPM. His plan was simple. Every two years, he would buy a house with a 5 percent down payment and move his family into it. Each time he moved his family into a new house, he would lease the previous residence. In the years he didn't move his family, he would buy another investment home with a 20 percent down payment. Twelve years later, he sold most of his fourteen houses, then put the $1.2 million of profit into syndicated real estate investments that yield 18 to 20 percent a year tax-free. (We'll talk more about syndicated real estate deals and how to lower your taxable income in Law Seventeen.)

That's how he could retire from *needing* to work. He now works on things he cares about instead of working out of obligation and necessity.

You can do the same. Starting out, it may seem like you need to take big risks to succeed. In reality, everyday people can build wealth by understanding and effectively using wealth-creation tools.

My wife got us $60K worth of credit card loans at 4.5 percent annual interest and then lent the money out in hundreds of microloans at 10 percent interest every two weeks. The cost of the $60K debt is $250 a month, and the profit (after delinquencies) averaged between $5K and $7K a month. Once the proof of concept was established, it wasn't hard to scale the lending amount and turn $7K monthly profit into $20K monthly profit, pay off the loan, and keep the cycle running indefinitely. It's not easy, but it is simple, and it's obtainable for anyone. As mentioned earlier, Derek earned a firefighter's salary and still made big things happen using small amounts of OPM. If he can do it, so can you.

Rethinking How We View Money

Most of us have preconceived notions about money, often shaped by our upbringing and experiences. These subconscious beliefs can be difficult to navigate once we reach adulthood. This mental baggage, combined with our limited experiences, shapes our perceptions of money and negatively affects how we use it. It's easy to develop a warped and incomplete understanding of money. In its simplest form, money is a resource, a tool like any other. Watching the experts use OPM effectively helps us see money in this way.

Consider the diverse financial behaviors and attitudes that result from different personal financial histories. Those who lived through the Great Depression, for instance, are known for their frugality and aversion to unnecessary spending. Individuals who grew up with limited resources may approach money differently than those raised in affluence.

Someone who grew up in a financially secure environment may view investing as a natural and essential part of life. In contrast, someone who experienced financial instability may view investing as risky and prefer to keep their money in safer, more liquid forms, such as cash or savings accounts. These unique experiences shape our financial behaviors and attitudes, which can either hinder or facilitate our economic growth.

Remember, money itself has no intrinsic value; it's just paper. If you were stranded on an island with all the money in the world, it would do you no good. The true value of money lies in its ability to give us access to tangible assets like property, goods, and services. It is a means to an end, not an end in itself. Therefore, the key to financial success is not to accumulate money based on its intrinsic value, but to use it as a tool to achieve our goals.

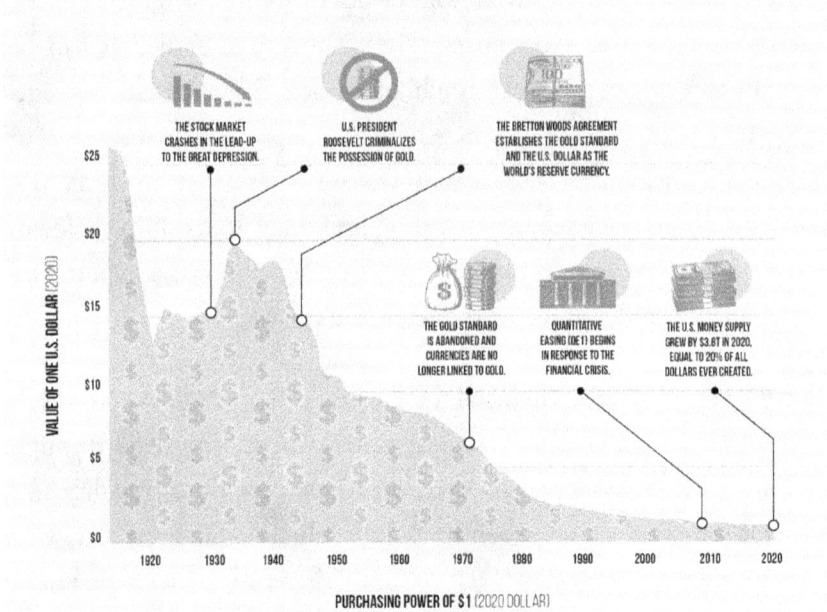

THE STOCK MARKET CRASHES IN THE LEAD-UP TO THE GREAT DEPRESSION.

U.S. PRESIDENT ROOSEVELT CRIMINALIZES THE POSSESSION OF GOLD.

THE BRETTON WOODS AGREEMENT ESTABLISHES THE GOLD STANDARD AND THE U.S. DOLLAR AS THE WORLD'S RESERVE CURRENCY.

THE GOLD STANDARD IS ABANDONED AND CURRENCIES ARE NO LONGER LINKED TO GOLD.

QUANTITATIVE EASING (QE 1) BEGINS IN RESPONSE TO THE FINANCIAL CRISIS.

THE U.S. MONEY SUPPLY GREW BY $3.8T IN 2020, EQUAL TO 20% OF ALL DOLLARS EVER CREATED.

VALUE OF ONE U.S. DOLLAR (2020)

PURCHASING POWER OF $1 (2020 DOLLAR)

Let me illustrate what I'm saying by showing you the purchasing power of the U.S. dollar. According to the Bureau of Labor Statistics, the purchasing power of the U.S. dollar is less than *half* of what it was when I was born in 1992 (thanks to inflation).

In fact, inflation has eroded the value of the dollar significantly over the past century. For example, $100 in 1920 could purchase $1,576 of goods and services in 2024. This means that over the course of a century, the value of the U.S. dollar has plummeted by 94 percent, losing nearly all its original purchasing power.[10]

The cash you hold loses a little more value every day, which means what it can buy you shrinks daily too. Most people don't consider this: If you save your money for long enough, it will evaporate in your hands like water. Inflation erodes the value of your paper money over time.

Let me explain this with a more vivid example that most of us can relate to—a candy bar. For our grandparents, a candy bar cost a nickel. Not too long ago, it was a dollar, and now it's $2.99 or more. The same amount of money that used to buy a candy bar is now insufficient to purchase even the smallest item. This is how inflation gradually erodes the value of money over time.

That's why protecting the value of your money is crucial for building wealth. One way to do this is to invest in tangible assets that are *not* subjected to currency devaluation. These assets, such as real estate, stocks, and precious metals, tend to appreciate over time, providing a safe hedge against inflation.

Imagine the potential if you had used *other people's money* thirty years ago, in 1994, to purchase a physical asset, such as a house, that you couldn't afford to pay for outright. Over the years, that asset would have appreciated in value as the U.S. dollar depreciated. You would have paid back your OPM and kept the appreciation. Even without including the income the asset would have generated, you would have made a substantial profit on someone else's money. If you had made a larger investment and included the income streams from the asset, your returns would be exceptional. When we invest with OPM, we're turning the negative effects of inflation to our advantage and opening up lucrative opportunities.

Assets are a powerful way to beat inflation, which is why the wealthy park their money in real assets like businesses, real estate, and stocks. But what if you took it one step further? By leveraging OPM, you can amplify your potential returns. OPM allows you to bet small and win big, removing the limitation of your savings and giving you access to investment opportunities with much higher returns. And even if you have the money, using OPM multiplies your wins. No matter how rich you are, you only have so much capital to work with. Your resources are limited; OPM is unlimited. This strategy allows you to maximize your investment potential and create significant wealth.

Now, I would never use OPM to buy stock because it is too inconsistent and the margins are not high enough to justify the risk, but I will use stocks in the next example to simplify how the money trail works.

Let's say you found a stock that *guaranteed* a 15 percent annual return and you had $100K of your own to invest. By the end of the year, your $100K would have grown to $115K, resulting in a $15K profit. Now, suppose you also leveraged $100K of OPM. This would bring your total investment pool to $200K, which would grow to $230K by the end of the year. Of this, $15K of the profit would come from your personal investment, while the other $15K would come from the leveraged funds.

If you paid your investors an 8 percent interest rate, you would owe $8K of the $15K profit, leaving you with a $7K profit from the OPM. Adding this to the $15K profit from your own funds brings your total profit to $22K. By using OPM, you not only increase your overall return, but you also accelerate your rate of return, even after accounting for the cost of borrowed funds.

That is the beauty of OPM.

Not All Opportunities Are Created Equal

I hope you're getting the hang of this by now! Using OPM amplifies your returns on opportunities when you may not have the capital to make it truly profitable, or when you want to add more to your capital, as we saw in the example above. That's exactly what many billionaires do. Leverage gives them exponential returns and accelerates their financial progress.

Warning: Using other people's money doesn't come *free*. (Pun intended.) OPM is an obligation. You take on a sizable risk when you borrow large amounts of OPM, so you must use it sparingly at first and be extremely wise with it.

Leveraging capital can amplify your losses if the investment goes south—which is why I mentioned earlier that I would never use OPM in the stock market. If a stock performs differently than you expect and makes only marginal returns, no returns, or goes south, you would not make *any* gains on your money. What's worse is that you'd have to repay the OPM you lost in its entirety, *with interest*. You should never use OPM on deals where success isn't inevitable.

You must choose investments with a high probability of success and substantial profit margins. Use OPM only for deals where literally everything would have to go wrong for you to lose money—where you know it's virtually impossible to lose. Finding ultrasafe investments takes a lot more work, but it's worth the effort.

People sometimes get tripped up when they use OPM for long-term investments that don't have immediate cash flow to support the debt.

Don't fall into this trap. Use this strategy only when your use of OPM has the cash flow to cover the debt and has substantial margins.

For example, it would be a bad idea to use OPM on a deal with a 20 percent IRR (internal rate of return) if the terms dictate that most of the profits will be received in five years, but you must cover the debt servicing fees now. This could lead to serious cash flow problems and potentially bankruptcy (even if the numbers work on paper).

To avoid potential cash flow issues, it's important to increase the margin of time between when you receive income from your investment and when you need to pay the fees associated with OPM. One effective way to do this is to negotiate terms that allow for deferred payments or interest-only periods in the early stages of the investment. This gives you more time to generate income from the investment before your repayment obligations kick in, giving you more control over your financial situation.

The key is to ensure you have plenty of margin with the necessary funds to cover the debt payments as they come due. When done properly, you should have plenty of room to leverage OPM effectively without jeopardizing your financial stability. Always prioritize investments that align with this strategy to maintain a healthy cash flow and maximize your returns.

This is also why, ironically, the wealthiest people are the ones who use OPM most effectively. Their healthy margins keep them safe while they leverage capital to multiply their returns.

So, if you don't have a lot of buffer, use OPM sparingly until you have enough margin to safely increase your leverage.

Use it as a Tool, Not a Crutch

OPM is such a powerful tool that many business owners are tempted to rely on it a little too heavily, and that's when they get into trouble. The key is to use it as a tool, not a crutch. When used strategically, OPM can fuel rapid growth, but it's not a shortcut to avoid the essential work of refining your business model and improving operational efficiency. It's important to strengthen the foundation of your business first, and then use OPM to grow it, not prop it up.

Before you consider leveraging OPM, make sure your business model can stand on its own merits. If your business isn't profitable without outside funding, OPM will only mask underlying problems. Once you have a profitable and scalable business model, leveraging other people's money becomes a powerful growth accelerator.

Here's what using OPM as a crutch might look like. Some entrepreneurs use OPM to scale their operations rapidly without ensuring their business model is sustainable. For example, a startup might raise large amounts of venture capital to expand into new markets and launch new products without validating that its fundamentals are truly profitable. (We will talk more about this in Law Seven.) This makes them look like geniuses until their business collapses when the external funding runs out.

If a department is struggling to keep up with demand, it may be easier to use OPM to hire more staff than to address the underlying problems behind the symptoms. Some may inadvertently use OPM to mask cash flow issues instead of addressing their sales and marketing challenges. Whatever the problems, OPM can provide temporary relief, but unfortunately it doesn't solve the underlying inefficiencies.

Simply put, the danger with OPM arises when it's used as a crutch for faltering business strategies, rather than as a catalyst for thriving business models. This misuse can lead to a downward spiral that undermines the very foundation of your business.

By avoiding these pitfalls and harnessing OPM responsibly, entrepreneurs can forge a robust, sustainable foundation for their businesses. They can leverage external funding not just to enhance their success, but to catapult it and open up a world of opportunity for growth and prosperity.

Start Small and Then Scale

When my wife and I first started leveraging other people's money, we used 0 percent interest credit card loans to renovate rental properties and then used the tenants' income to repay the loan. Home renovation loans can also be a great source of OPM because they typically have low interest rates and are easy to obtain without the red tape associated with mortgages or business loans. Although it's not infinitely scalable, this could be a good place to start using OPM. Remember, as long as the income is coming in *because of* the OPM, you should be in a good spot.

Another way to start small with OPM is to buy small rental properties with OPM from friends and family. You could start by purchasing a single-family home or duplex using a low-interest personal loan or home equity line of credit (HELOC). The beauty of this strategy is that rental income from tenants can be used to cover the loan payments, creating a steady cash flow while you build equity in the property. Once you have a proven track record with one or two properties, it's much easier to ask friends and family to invest with you.

Another viable option is to invest in laundromats. These businesses are relatively low-maintenance and can generate consistent revenue. Here's one way to do it: Use a small business loan or equipment financing to cover the initial costs. Then use the income from the laundromat operations to pay off the loan. It's a straightforward process that can yield significant returns, along with some of the most incredible tax incentives (which we'll discuss in detail in Law Seventeen).

Similarly, vending machine businesses offer a low-cost entry into entrepreneurship. You can start generating income quickly by using a small loan to purchase a few vending machines and placing them in high-traffic areas. The income from the machines can pay off the loan and help you continue to expand your vending network.

By starting small with these methods and scaling up as you gain experience and success, you can effectively use OPM to expand your investments and business ventures. This strategy can lead to significant growth and success without overextending yourself financially.

And that's where the real work begins. *Stand on the shoulders of giants* by surrounding yourself with people who are already investing in the areas you want to pursue. Learn their strategies, and then use OPM to maximize your results. The key to using leverage successfully is to stick with it long enough to find applications that consistently work. Once you've successfully identified an investment that uses leveraged capital, you can scale it infinitely.

As I've shown, OPM can be applied to opportunities across various asset classes. Leveraging money (or time, as we'll see in the next chapter) multiplies your returns exponentially. That's what this book is all about! Identify one way you can start using it and start leveraging OPM now.

Reality Check:

Are your limited resources holding you back?

So, how do you start leveraging other people's money?

I recommend starting small. Try to find investment opportunities that offer higher returns than your borrowing costs. For example, find any real estate investment with a high probability of return and look for loans with lower interest rates to fund it. Classic assets like rental properties can be a good place to start, but many people have found success buying laundromats, car washes, established businesses, ATMs, vending machines, and other sources of recurring revenue.

Your investment should cash-flow at or before the payments for the borrowed funds begin. Ideally, you should find investments that pay you in the first month, but if that's not possible, find OPM where you can defer the first payment to make sure you have plenty of financial margin in case things don't go according to plan.

Once you've successfully used OPM and are comfortable turning a profit on a small scale, try using OPM on a larger scale to buy additional monthly income. If you already own a successful business, there may be opportunities to increase your cash flow by leveraging OPM to expand marketing efforts, open new offices, and hire more employees to increase production.

If your business is consistently profitable, find ways of using OPM that increase the output of services and, therefore, your profitability.

Start small to prove the concept, and then scale infinitely.

Leveraged Action Steps

	Leveraged Action Steps	Your Notes
#1	**Identify Potential Opportunities:** Name two ways you could increase your business or investment profits with OPM.	
#2	**Find Affordable Capital:** Find three low-cost borrowing options like credit card offers, home renovation loans, or funding from friends and family.	

#3	Invest Wisely and Keep Profits: Use the borrowed capital to invest and keep the leveraged profits.	

Chapter Two Takeaway

LAW TWO

LEVERAGE OTHER PEOPLE'S MONEY (OPM)

IN SMART AND RESPONSIBLE WAYS TO

EXPONENTIALLY INCREASE YOUR WEALTH.

Use Other People's Time (OPT)

"Do what you do best, and delegate the rest."

—Chris Ducker (serial entrepreneur and author)

Law Two focused on using other people's money to multiply your wealth. Let's build on that concept by finding ways to leverage other people's time. Many of you are likely already using this principle without even realizing it, as *leveraging OPT* is one of the most naturally occuring forms of leverage. And like many things in life, once you become aware how you're leveraging OPT, you can use it more effectively.

Time is the most valuable resource we have because it's the most finite. Whenever you delegate work to others, you're using their time, not your own. And when done properly, it's a win-win for both parties involved.

When I was in college, I realized I was spending too much time on tasks that didn't contribute to my education, like compiling facts instead of actually understanding them. To solve this, I organized groups of ten people and divided the research into five parts, with two people working independently on each subject. This way, each person only had to handle 20 percent of the research, and having two people complete each part ensured the data was accurate. This method allowed us to complete the assignments faster and produce better results.

Some may call this cheating, but the reality is that we weren't graded on how well we compiled information, but on how well we understood the concepts. Everyone in the group benefited from this arrangement; it was a win-win situation that optimized our time and effort. As I became more comfortable with delegation, I found myself using this strategy more often, freeing up valuable time to focus on studying for exams.

If you are in college, you may find this method helpful. Instead of waiting for the assignments to pile up and stressing yourself out over them, you could start delegating some of the busy work to your classmates. Or you could hire a tutor to help you with difficult parts so you can learn faster.

I'll give you another everyday example, for those of us who are no longer in an academic setting.

Let's say you're the primary caretaker for your family, with an overwhelming amount of responsibilities. You've got meals to prepare, laundry to wash, a lawn to keep up with, home décor to update, taxes to finish, and a million other things that *must* be done. At some point, you inadvertently decided to do all of it by yourself. Even if you pretend that you're superhuman, your time and energy *are* limited. By the time you've completed all your tasks, you realize that investing in your children—the most important thing to you—has taken a back seat. If you're not careful, you could spend 80 percent of your time doing things that *need* to happen but aren't truly *important,* and only 20 percent on the stuff that really matters.

But that doesn't need to be the case indefinitely. You could leverage OPT to delegate the most draining of these "80 percent" tasks so you can reserve your energy for the most important "20 percent" tasks (more on this soon).

This might be a difficult concept to wrap your head around at first. After all, you're used to handling everything yourself. You want it done right. You want it done fast. But the bottom line is this: Leveraging OPT is the only surefire way to be certain that you get to devote your attention to the projects and moments that matter most.

That's what the third law is about: Leveraging other people's time. Your ability to outsource tasks and delegate responsibilities is crucial in reclaiming the limited time you have and channeling that time into higher leverage activities (such as investing time with your children, expanding your business, acquiring assets, or improving your health). Using your time on the highest leverage activities puts you at a massive advantage.

Still not convinced that delegation is the best strategy? Consider the following scenarios and see if they don't change your mind about the value of leveraging other people's time.

Business owner "A" spends his time managing the day-to-day operations of his company. He's bogged down with paperwork, employee management, and other tedious tasks, spending over forty hours a week just keeping things running.

Business owner "B" outsources and delegates those same responsibilities to others while supervising the results. This allows her to focus on product development, client acquisition, and raising capital.

Business owner "A" is doing everything himself, while business owner "B" is focusing on the tasks only she can do.

Which venture do you think will be more profitable? Nine times out of ten, it's business owner "B." That's the power of correctly using OPT.

The 80/20 Rule

To maximize your limited time, you must identify and prioritize the most important tasks over the never-ending to-do list. Offloading repetitive work so you can focus on more valuable tasks is a critical piece of applying this law correctly.

Our lives are complex and multifaceted. We all have a lot on our plates, some of which we volunteered for and many tasks we did not. Life has a way of thrusting an ever-growing pile of projects, responsibilities, and tasks onto us. As adults, there is a nearly infinite list of things we need to get done along with the goals and dreams we want to transform into reality. Thankfully, there are some principles that can help us get there.

In fact, there's one rule that will help you more than any other. This rule is called the Pareto Principle, or the 80/20 rule, which states that 80 percent of our results come from only 20 percent of our efforts. Suppose you're trying to improve your health; if you compare your activities to your results, you might discover that 20 percent of your efforts (such as cutting sugar from your diet or scheduling regular exercise) are responsible for 80 percent of your progress. Once you determine what fuels your results, you can achieve more efficient outcomes by prioritizing those activities and eliminating the rest.

In other words, focusing your energy and resources on the significant 20 percent of your inputs will yield 80 percent of your results. The key, then, is to identify and prioritize the most impactful 20 percent of tasks, rather than tackling 100 percent of the tasks on our docket.

The 80/20 rule is a powerful tool that can be applied to all areas of life to help you make the most effective decisions. In a world of unlimited options, it's easy to lose sight of the most important tasks. This rule provides clarity and helps you choose the options that align with your best self and deliver the greatest value.

As an entrepreneur or leader, your ultimate focus is most likely on revenue and profit. Some may shy away from admitting it, but it's the truth. If you don't focus on revenue and profit, you might not have the capital to help very many people. That means it's time to concentrate on the activities that increase those numbers. So, what if you *only* spent time on the 20 percent of activities that directly drive revenue and offloaded the remaining 80 percent of the work to others? Most businesses do this, whether they realize it or not. That's why you see so many secretaries, virtual assistents, and interns—they handle the income generators' scheduling, accounting, and facility management. This allows the leader to focus on strategy, sales, marketing, and business development—the high-leverage activities that directly impact their numbers. This is a typical example of leveraging OPT.

In the workplace, you can use the 80/20 rule to improve your productivity by focusing on the top 20 percent of tasks and delegating the less important ones. Furthermore, analyzing the current efforts and processes responsible for most of your results will help you improve your systems and lead to wiser decision-making, yielding better outcomes.

Applying the 80/20 rule to your personal relationships can also bring a sense of freedom. Instead of spreading yourself thin and attempting to please everyone, focus on deepening your connections with the most important people in your life. You'll find a significant improvement in your well-being and happiness when you reduce the time and energy you devote to the 80 percent of activities and conversations that drain you.

Consider the practicality of this rule in your everyday life, even if you don't own a business. Think about how often you outsource tasks without realizing it. For instance, when your car breaks down, you probably call a mechanic instead of trying to fix it yourself. You *could* spend endless hours attempting the repair, but it's far more efficient to pay someone who can have it done by dinnertime. This is the 80/20 rule in action—focusing on what you do best and outsourcing the rest.

Getting Started With Leveraging OPT

As you begin to look for ways to conserve your time, you'll find that there are endless ways to apply the third law of leverage to your daily life. This will hopefully lead to a massive increase in the amount of time you can devote to your most important projects.

Here are just a few ways to get you started.

Hire a helper to cook your meals at your home; they can even shop for the ingredients, meal prep, pack it all in Tupperware, and clean up once they're done.

Outsourcing tasks is simpler than you might think. Here's how I hired my cook. I found a website for freelance maids and asked three of them if they would be willing to shop and cook for me at their requested $15-an-hour rate. Remember, this was a cleaning service, not a cooking service. Within an hour of searching, I found and hired the cook I used for the next two years.

This is how the math plays out. By hiring a cook by the hour (as opposed to a full-time helper), I was limiting the cost to $100 a week ($5,200 a year). Outsourcing my meals freed up roughly 520 hours of my time and allowed me to reclaim the mental capacity I needed to focus on tasks that make ten to twenty times that per hour.

To make your food outsourcing even easier, consider buying ready-made meals at Costco. It might cost you an extra $100 to $200 a week, but you can channel that time into higher leverage activities that will more than cover your expense. The entrepreneur Alex Hormozi did a similar thing and outsourced his meals to Chipotle, Panda Express, and Chick-fil-A. He spent $600 to $700 a week outsourcing his food and used that time to focus on the work *only he could do* in building his $100 million gym business. (P.S., Alex is a true health nut and would carefully select only the healthiest options.)[11]

If you enjoy cooking and are good at it, this might not be the first task you outsource—but you can always use the same thought process for other everyday activities you *do* hate wasting time on.

Hire a lawn crew and reclaim your mowing or trimming hours. Even better, hire a local teenager to come once a week to clean your home, mow your lawn, and handle the home maintenance tasks that drain you. It'll be a win-win, and you'll help someone else in the process. Many high-schoolers will jump at the opportunity for any work that comes their way, especially if you *overpay* them. It gives them extra income and the real-world experience they'll need to excel later on.

If you're not in a position to pay for help, there are still ways to leverage OPT. Consider swapping tasks with friends or family. This not only allows you to tap into their skills but also empowers you to offer your own expertise. If you're great at graphic design and your friend excels at home maintenance, offer to design marketing materials for them in exchange for their repairing that leaky faucet. Both of you will benefit by focusing on your strengths and offloading tasks you're less efficient at.

Another approach is to participate in time-banking communities. Time banking is not just about exchanging services; it's about building a network of support within your community. You could offer an hour of tutoring in a subject you're knowledgeable about in exchange for an hour of babysitting. This allows you to leverage others' skills without spending money, while also fostering a sense of community and connection.

Look for opportunities to join or form cooperative groups. Childcare co-ops are a great example where parents share the responsibility of watching each other's children. You could arrange a schedule where each parent takes a turn watching the group of children, freeing up time for the others to focus on their own tasks. Similarly, carpooling with neighbors can save time and reduce commuting stress.

Another option is to look for community resources. Many local organizations offer free or low-cost services. Community centers often host volunteer groups willing to help with yard work or local kitchens that provide meal prep assistance. Libraries frequently run tutoring programs where you can swap skills, like teaching English, in exchange for help with your taxes. Additionally, check out local online forums or social media groups where people often offer free services or skill swaps.

Recognizing your time wasters and redirecting that energy is a mindset shift that can radically improve your life. By strategically leveraging OPT, you can free up significant time and mental bandwidth to focus on what truly matters. So, why not start today? Identify one task you can outsource and see the difference it makes in your productivity.

Getting Used to Leveraging OPT

Changing your mindset is the key to altering any well-established pattern in your life. This advice is likely something you have heard often over the years, and like most frequently cited manners of thought, there is a lot of truth to be found in it.

If you're not used to systematizing and delegating everything you do, it might initially feel scary and awkward. You may even feel guilty outsourcing low-leverage tasks so you can make more by doubling down on the higher leverage activities. It's important to remember that you aren't "pushing tasks onto someone else" out of a sense of laziness—quite the opposite. You're delegating these tasks to buy back your time to work on the most valuable projects for your mission.

As you buy back your time, you'll get a lot further with less stress. And even better, you will get there faster than you ever would have utilizing just your own time. We live in a world where outsourcing is easier than ever before because everything is more interconnected. Taskrabbit, PeoplePerHour, Fiverr, Freelancer, and Upwork are all examples of sites that offer help with everything from handyman services to graphic design, bookkeeping, virtual assistance, and customer service. These sites revolve around offering you solutions for outsourcing the 80 percent.

Time is your most valuable asset, and you can't get it back once it's gone. Stop wasting it on tasks you can easily outsource. Treat your personal life like a business: Hire people to take care of your cooking, cleaning, laundry, and any task that can help free up time and energy for the most essential things in your personal life. For some, this will be focused on the business; for others, this means spending quality time with loved ones or pursuing your passions; for others still, it may be getting into the best shape of your life. The point is, when you use OPT, you make the best use of your time. If you want an extraordinary life, you must implement extraordinary strategies. That's the whole point of these eighteen laws.

I don't want to overwhelm you as you implement strategies for the first time. So as always, my advice is to start small. Outsource a few small tasks and see how they go. As you become more comfortable with delegation, you can scale up. Remember to remain organized; have a schedule for the tasks you're outsourcing so you can track them effectively. Anticipate where you'll need help, and plan accordingly in advance.

Things You Should *Not* Delegate

Using other people's time is a great way to eliminate the aspects of your life or career that are bogging you down and stalling your progress. But it makes sense *not* to delegate certain things. Just as you wouldn't hand over your most valuable assets to strangers, certain responsibilities should remain under your control.

As a founder or company leader, for example, don't delegate things that would compromise the confidential aspects of your business or anything that depends on your specific talent. While routine tasks can and should be delegated, it's crucial to personally manage key responsibilities like shaping company culture and safeguarding strategic intellectual property. These areas directly impact the core direction and values of your organization and benefit from your direct involvement and leadership.

Take full responsibility for your personal finances. While I strongly encourage hiring coaches, tax planners, and other investment partners, managing your finances is a task that shouldn't be delegated. Ultimately, it requires your own time, attention, and focus.

These are foundations that need to be personally managed. It's important to make this distinction when determining which tasks can be performed by employees and which are for your eyes only.

The great thing is that when you have delegated everything that should be outsourced, you'll have a wealth of time and energy to invest in the important things.

Reality Check:

Are the details holding you back?

It's easy to get bogged down in the specifics of outsourcing. Fear of losing control, concerns about work quality, and the effort to find the right person can all be paralyzing. But remember, leveraging other people's time is about liberating yourself from low-value tasks to free up your energy to focus on the things that truly matter.

Don't overthink it.

Don't worry about the perfect way to delegate, the ideal person to hire, or the best platform to use. The key to overcoming decision paralysis is to start small and keep it simple. You can always adjust and refine your approach as you go, but the most important step is to begin. Overthinking will only delay the advantages you can gain from using OPT. So, start small, keep it simple, and watch your efficiency and happiness soar.

Identify one low-leverage task you hate doing and outsource it.

It could be something as simple as grocery shopping, cleaning, or routine administrative work. Find a reliable service or individual to take over this task. By starting with just one task, you'll quickly see the benefits of outsourcing and become more comfortable with the process.

This small step can lead to significant improvements in your productivity and overall satisfaction.

Outsource one task this week and enjoy the results.

Leveraged Action Steps

	Leveraged Action Steps	Your Notes
#1	**Identify High-Leverage Activities:** What tasks drive the highest return for you?	
#2	**List Tasks for Delegation:** Which tasks are you most comfortable delegating?	
#3	**Outsource a Task:** Choose one small task to outsource this week.	

#4	**Communicate Clearly:** When delegating, be clear about your expectations. Prepare a one-page task sheet detailing the procedures, timeline, and compensation.	

Chapter Three Takeaway

LAW THREE
TIME IS OUR MOST VALUABLE RESOURCE, SO LEVERAGE OTHER PEOPLE'S TIME (OPT) SO YOU CAN FOCUS ON THE HIGHEST LEVERAGE ACTIVITIES AND SUCCEED FASTER.

Charge for the Result; Hire by the Hour

"The most powerful force in the world of business is not technology, money, or innovation—it's trust."

—Stephen Covey (author, The 7 Habits of Highly Effective People)

Money talks. Price tags talk too. Have you ever wondered why someone like Tony Robbins charges anywhere from $20K to $80K to get people's lives back on track, while your local shrink charges $100 to $150 an hour to accomplish the same thing? If you don't know the ins and outs of Law Four, it might mystify you that a guru like Tony Robbins will sell out an entire room and charge each attendee thousands of dollars per hour, while another professional may provide a similar service and struggle to find clients even if they're offering their services at a fraction of the cost.

This concept might seem strange, but it's actually very common. It's part of a fascinating phenomenon in a world of free market capitalism, where the price of a product or service can vary widely, depending on how it's packaged and positioned. Most people have an innate desire to choose the cheapest option and yet will be willing to pay ten times the ongoing market rate—*if* what they want to buy is sold to them in a specific way.

If you think about this closely enough, you'll find this principle is actively at work in almost every industry. A well-known plumbing company may charge a flat $3K fee for a project, while your local handyman charges $20 to $40 per hour. If you compared the end result of the two, you might only pay the hourly worker half what you would pay the corporation. Similarly, a professional chef may charge $1K a week to cook your meals, while a meal prep company will charge somewhere around $200 per person per week, and a maid for hire will charge $10 to $15 per hour to do the same work.

Now, there certainly may be a difference in the quality of service provided in each of those options, but the point is that when we're choosing to buy something, we're not just responding to the offering itself, but also—in a very big way—to the positioning. As the author Stephen Covey illustrates, *trust* is the most powerful force in business; it's the promise and comprehensiveness of the solution we're buying. In many cases, we exhibit more trust in the larger, fancier packages because the positioning dictates it as being of high excellence and experience. The product's or service's positioning has created a high level of trust, and we, as clients and consumers, are drawn to that.

The best businesses understand this. They know building trust with their clientele and perfecting their positioning can make a world of difference in how their product sells. I've discovered that the wealthiest and most successful people charge for the end result or desired *outcome* of their products and services, while the little guys will charge for their *time*.

That brings us to our next law of leverage: Charge for the result, and in order to deliver that result, hire by the hour.

Are You *Using* Leverage or *Being* Leveraged?

Seeing this particular law of leverage in action isn't always pleasant. I won't sugarcoat it: As you read this, you might realize that you're the one being leveraged, rather than the one using leverage for your own benefit.

Most companies charge their clients a set figure and then pay their employees hourly. Hiring by the hour is generally much cheaper than paying for a completed project, so the difference between those two numbers is the firm's profit—that's how most businesses work. Unfortunately, this means most hourly employees are getting the short end of the stick, and this very well may include *you*.

In my last book, *Crush Your Kryptonite*, I discussed the brutal reality that very few of the top 5 percent of income earners have a fixed salary or an hourly wage. Instead, most ultrahigh earners understand this law of leverage and establish a different source (or, even more often, multiple sources) of income. They build their own businesses or personal brands instead of accepting a salary or an hourly wage. Another way to do this is through sales positions and commission-based roles, where you control the leverage instead of *being* the leverage. If you're compensated for the results you create, you'll earn significantly more than an hourly rate.

A professional brand with a solid reputation is able to set a price for a result because they have consumer *trust*. Their positioning serves as a lantern, drawing the buyer in. They earn people's business and then find ways to outsource some of that work—becoming wealthy in the process.

The larger a company is, the more they have to underpay those they employ because of the many variables and uncertainties they are mitigating.

If you work for a large organization, the reason *you* might not earn what you want is because your employer is charging for the product/service and then paying you by the hour. In other words, *you're* the leverage they're building their company with. Sadly, this is especially true if you're above average in competency for the task you were hired for. In fact, when you're an hourly employee, the better you are at your job, the greater your loss is financially. This is because the company you work for has to maintain a profit on every transaction while subsidizing the lackluster results from other employees that are below average in competency for the task they were hired for.

In other words, for many reasons, you're getting underpaid for your level of expertise while someone else is getting overpaid for their lack of expertise, and the company is getting compensated for the trust of their brand. Sorry, but you're the one losing out here every single time.

If this chapter bursts your bubble, this is a good thing. Now that you're aware of how you are being leveraged, and what you're losing in the process, you can start changing the way you're compensated. Once you understand how to *charge for the result*, you'll see that the world of leverage presents you with two distinct roles: you're either harnessing leverage, or becoming leverage for someone else. The contrast between these roles is stark. It's obvious which of those roles most people end up in—but it's also obvious which role most people would like to be in.

The one harnessing leverage is the master of their own destiny. They set high prices based on the value they provide. They are constantly learning, taking calculated risks, growing outside their comfort zones, and building meaningful relationships as they make a difference in people's lives. The one who harnesses leverage leads a life of adventure, gets to pursue their passions, and makes a difference in the world.

On the other hand, the leveraged typically live with golden handcuffs. Stable jobs and regular paychecks may be more comfortable in the short term, but the trade-off for giving up freedom, losing control over time, and depending on others for rewards, is often an unfulfilling life in the long run.

So I challenge you to ask yourself: Who do you want to be? Let this be a call to action to take control of your life and future.

You have two choices: You can use this knowledge to become a leverager or you can remain the leveraged.

Doubling Down on OPT

Law Three, use other people's time (OPT), was all about delegating work to others so that you can make the most of your time.

When you charge for a project (aka the result) and outsource work by the hour, you can double down on what you are best at to expand your business faster. So if you're good at what you do and people know it, feel free to leverage that specific expertise to grow your business.

Outsource tasks that aren't your specialty and watch your success multiply.

Creating Win-Wins

A company recently hired me for a $2K sound engineering project. I then hired two sound engineers at $30 an hour for a total of thirty-five hours, paid them $1,050 for their labor, and kept the remaining $950. I can do this because I was a sound engineer for many years, and even though I've been out of the business for a while, I still get the occasional gig from a company or musician who needs help. When I do, I take the job and outsource it to friends in the business.

This kind of collaboration works because it's a win-win for everyone involved. Not everyone loves sales and marketing. Even the most talented people can't be good at everything, nor do they have the bandwidth to manage everything proficiently. This creates opportunities for the leverager.

People want different things out of their lives and work, which creates opportunity for those who can connect the pieces of the puzzle. Connecting workers to customers is both fulfilling and profitable. This involves identifying the results customers are willing to pay for and matching them with the skills and services of workers. In the earlier example, my sound engineer friends are genuinely grateful when I send them work. Many contractors and subcontractors know they are making pennies on the dollar, but they prefer to stay in their lane and are happy to leave the sales and marketing to someone else.

This is where the opportunity lies for those of us who understand Law Four.

Law Four teaches us the power of building a trusted brand. Those who are motivated to do so are happy to reach a position where they can continually charge for their project, result, brand, or name.

If you want to be a leverager, find people who are happy to be leveraged in return for fair compensation and build the best win-wins. Remember, the people you're leveraging are also leveraging you.

I can give you loads of examples. Tom Clancy, one of the best spy authors ever, is dead[12] but still writes best-selling books! His readers, avid fans of the fictional protagonist, CIA-turned-President Jack Ryan, can't get enough of the thrillers. While *The Teeth of the Tiger* was Clancy's last book with his name as the only author on the cover, we've now seen Jack Ryan hit the bookstores again, written by Tom Clancy with XYZ.

Command Authority was launched a year after Clancy's death and was co-authored with Mark Greaney. Other co-authors include Grant Blackwood, Peter Telep, and perhaps more—they're all writers who've been happy to collaborate with Clancy for many years now. What I'm trying to say here is that the brand name "Clancy," which was built many years ago, lives on and continues to attract readers, even though the writing is someone else's—everyone wins.[13]

You'll see the same happening in the fashion world. Fashion influencers invest heavily in cultivating a dedicated audience and establishing their distinctive brand. Then, they leverage these brands to generate revenue through sponsored posts, advertisements, and affiliate income. Once their brands are established, influencers often launch their own clothing or makeup lines. However, they are typically not these products' primary manufacturers or designers. Most influencers are "white-labeling" products, meaning they resell items someone else manufactures under their label. This is a win-win because it's much more likely for someone to purchase a high-end dress from a celebrity brand than from an unknown manufacturer in a country they've never been to. So, the influencers leverage the manufacturers' infrastructure, and the manufacturers leverage the publicity of the brands.

When leveragers find the right partnerships, the rewards are windfalls. Think of Apple! Apple outsources its production to three big manufacturers: Foxconn, Pegatron, and Wistron. Apple has created so much demand that all three contractors continuously expand their manufacturing endeavors to keep up with the demand.[14] If this isn't a win-win, I don't know what is. Nike does something similar and outsources its production to roughly 600 manufacturing companies worldwide to divvy up the workload and optimize for productivity. This strategy allows Nike to leverage the cost advantages, skilled labor, and infrastructure capabilities of different regions, ensuring efficiency and a steady supply to meet global demand. And look at the sort of love (and money) Nike gets from its customers. Again, a win-win for all.

The good news is that you don't have to reach the scale of Apple or Nike to harness this form of leverage. Anyone can embrace this fundamental principle: Identify a service people are willing to pay for and outsource it for less than you charge. By doing so, your clients receive top-notch service, your suppliers or employees will receive fair compensation, and you, in turn, generate a nice margin without shouldering the entire workload yourself. The added beauty of this approach is that it will open up new opportunities for scale that might never have been possible if you were solely responsible for all aspects of customer fulfillment.

However you do it, once you set up your systems to cater to the demand while outsourcing the work, there's a *lot* of money to be made.

The Power of the Brand

Let's go back to the example of Tony Robbins and your local therapist. The key distinction between them is the personal brand that Tony Robbins has meticulously built. While many people are familiar with Tony Robbins, the same cannot be said for your local therapist. This lack of brand recognition significantly affects their respective levels of influence and success.

To harness Law Four, you'll need to build and unleash the power of your own brand.

Pause for a moment to reflect on the brands you love the most. What is it about them that you love? Sure, the product or service has got to be great. But why do you love that particular brand and not the thousands of others with the same product or service?

My guess is that some part of your answer is because you trust them more than the other options. You know that they have quality products or services. This knowledge forms a safety net beneath you; it allows you to justify spending the extra cash because you feel secure in the end result that you'll receive. The opposite scenario—a name you aren't familiar with—breeds reservations, hesitations, and potentially distrust. It means you will want to spend less for the product or service when you can't be certain of the quality you'll get.

Transparency is a cornerstone in the purchasing habits of millennials and Gen Zers, with trust being even more crucial now than it was for previous generations. We live in an era of abundant, easily accessible information, where every company is scrutinized online through reviews and customer experiences. This landscape has led us to disproportionately allocate our spending to companies with top-tier reputations while overlooking those with average results and online visibility.

We prefer to spend money with companies we feel like we know, and the companies that prioritize their online images the best are frequently the ones collecting the most cash.

Organizations that understand this shift in consumer behavior can successfully apply Law Four: charging clients for the brand's promise while outsourcing by the hour. This strategy works because consumers trust the brand to deliver without worrying about how the service is provided. We usually don't know or care where or how a company fulfills its products; we just care about the results.

The Magic of Outsourcing by the Hour

I first discovered the fourth law of leverage while renovating our beloved 1920s home in Dallas, Texas. That was when I discovered the sheer simplicity and power of bidding for a project and then outsourcing the work by the hour.

My wife and I love the charm of older homes and jumped at the opportunity to restore this treasure to its former glory, despite the numerous challenges that such a purchase entails. It was a chaotic but passionate endeavor, fueled by our appreciation for the unique architecture and the rarity of these houses in our city.

The foundation and structural integrity of the home needed to be resolved before any other projects could be tackled, so we sought the help of a reputable foundation company. They sent their hotshot sales guy in a bright red polo to explain the work needed, timeline, and cost. They were reputable and professional, so we hired them.

A team of twelve men arrived a few weeks later to begin working on our house. While conversing with the workers, I realized they were subcontractors rather than direct employees of the foundation company we hired. They were an independent team contracted by several foundation companies in the area. The big business handled the process of securing the jobs, then the subcontractors took care of the hands-on labor.

After completing the job, the sales guy, who was the liaison between us and the subcontractors, returned to ensure the crew had finished their work and that we were satisfied. Boom. Transaction complete on all three sides.

That's when I realized what the foundation company had gotten so right. We have a finite number of things we can devote our time and attention to. The company had chosen to invest its limited mental capacity on the highest leverage activity, which was building a trustworthy brand (and not on the actual work of foundation repairs). Building a prominent brand in a competitive city is much more profitable than the actual service they were selling, and by outsourcing most work to independent contractors, they could leverage their brand to expand exponentially.

As our renovation continued, there was a recurring pattern that caught my attention: Every time I requested a quote for a task—whether it involved repairing rotten siding, constructing a deck, or painting—

the quoted costs were consistently higher for companies that charged for the result, versus the handymen that charged for their time. The price varied based on the positioning of the service.

The next time I embarked on a foundation project for another house, I sought an hourly quote instead. I had paid $20K for the previous job, but this time the quote came in at $30 per hour for 96 hours of work plus $2,000 for supplies, totaling just $4,880! Embracing the approach of conducting thorough due diligence and being open to hiring a lesser-known subcontractor has allowed us to accomplish projects at a fraction of the cost. But while we were comfortable with the messy process, we acknowledged that most homeowners may not want to engage in the legwork of scrutinizing subcontractors. Most buyers prefer well-known, trusted brands, even if it means paying a premium for their services. These brands often charge four to five times higher fees, but buyers are willing to pay for the convenience and peace of mind they offer. Our revelation had been made.

Our experience serves as a testament to the fourth law of leverage. It's a reminder that where there is a brand, there's trust—and where there's trust, there can be leverage.

Reality Check:

Do you charge for the result?

For those of you who aren't quite ready to charge for the result and hire by the hour, here's one way you can apply the first half of this law.

It's time to look under the hood of your pricing model to find areas for improvement.

Let's start with your side hustle income.

If you're skilled at something and charging by the hour, it's time to make a change. Say a neighbor or acquaintance wants to hire you. Instead of quoting your hourly rate, estimate how many hours the project will take and multiply that by twice your previous hourly rate—quote that total price. This is the number you will quote from now on. You may be pleasantly surprised at how many people say yes.

Here's a simple rule of thumb for pricing: If everyone readily agrees to your rate, you're undercharging.

If you're worried about losing clients when you raise your rates, here's a new way to think about it: If you lose half your clients, you'll still make the same amount of money for half the work. This allows you to focus on delivering quality over quantity, reducing stress, and hopefully increasing satisfaction for both you and your clients.

By charging more, you're positioning yourself as a high-value service provider and attracting clients who are willing to pay for your expertise.

Remember, when someone hires you, they're not just paying for your time; they're paying for the time they would have spent learning a new skill and doing the work themselves. Your fees should reflect more than just the time spent on the task, and should include the effort you've invested in mastering the skill, along with the cost of any tools needed to complete the job. Understanding this can help you feel more confident about raising your prices.

Just start—and keep at it. With each step, you'll get closer to charging what you're really worth and, ultimately, to achieving the leverage you desire.

Leveraged Action Steps

I've given you many ways to apply Law Four. Now it's your turn to pick (or create) one of your own. List three examples where you can leverage your strengths by charging for your brand and outsourcing the work by the hour.

	Leveraged Action Steps	Your Notes
#1	**Website Design:** Build a website design company. Charge for the result, outsource the work overseas, and keep the spread.	
#2	**Design Agency:** Act as the intermediary between clients and designers. Secure clients and outsource design projects to trusted artists, earning a margin on each project.	
#3	**Virtual Assistant Agency:** Build a virtual assistant brand. Charge for service and outsource to VAs around the globe.	

#4	White Label Deals:	
	Find valuable products and services and resell them for 20–40 percent more. Change the name to match your brand and offer it to your current customer base.	

Chapter Four Takeaway

LAW FOUR

CHARGE FOR THE RESULT, OUTSOURCE WORK
BY THE HOUR, AND KEEP THE DIFFERENCE.

Charge for Your Brand to Build Your Brand

"You're not going to get rich renting out your time. You must own equity—a piece of a business—to gain your financial freedom."

—Naval Ravikant (angel investor and author)

Music is a cutthroat business. Think about how quickly some artists skyrocket into the Top 40 charts, only to fade from the spotlight just as quickly. Many musical artists are willing to sacrifice just about anything to stay in the limelight. Despite this being the industry's main goal, few have truly cracked the code to consistent domination. Ariana Grande is a prime example of someone who has; she remained at the top of the industry from 2013 to 2023, and is poised to dominate even longer if she chooses. We'll circle back to how she's achieved this in a moment.

A lot of people mistakenly assume that the best artists are the ones who make it to the top and *then* become the most profitable. I disagree; I think it's the profitable music acts that have the capital to be able to stay at the top, not the other way around. It's profit first, then fame—not fame, then profit.

Look at it this way. If two countries go to war, who do you think will win nine times out of ten? It will most likely be the country that can afford to finance the war effort the longest. History has proven this many times. Take the American Revolution, for example. Despite initial disadvantages, the American colonies eventually received significant financial and military support from France. This support was crucial in turning the tide against the British, who eventually ran out of funding.[15] Without substantial financial backing, the outcome could have been very different. Something similar happened during World War II. The Allies had superior economic resources and industrial capacity, which were critical to their victory over the Axis powers (Germany, Italy, and Japan). The United States, in particular, ramped up its production capabilities, supplying vast amounts of weapons, vehicles, and supplies to Allied forces.

These examples demonstrate that money is often an unspoken but decisive factor in determining the outcome of wars. Funding enables sustained military efforts, superior technology, and better-equipped forces, ultimately tipping the scales in favor of the financially stronger side.

The music business functions in exactly the same way. Famous music acts don't just happen, or at least, they rarely do. Sure, there's a talented artist involved, but the most successful music acts happen because someone leverages their resources to *market* the music hard enough to make a wave in people's day-to-day lives, and for long enough to garnish worldwide attention. Several studies have shown that the cost of promoting a song enough to get it into the Billboard Top 40s is over a million dollars.[16] That's a lot of money, and very few new musicians have the capital to make it happen. That's where the *starving artist* imagery comes from, and why music labels used to play such a pivotal role in an artist's career. Back in the day (and to a lesser extent, today), giant record labels would fund starving artists' careers and pay for the exposure they needed until they started turning a profit.

Here's where it gets tricky. Let's say a label is confident that a $2 million investment in promoting a new artist will yield a $3 million return. Even though they would recoup their investment and make a healthy profit for both parties, the label would need to take the lion's share of the profit to make it worthwhile. That's because they're the ones holding all the cards. They're the ones putting their capital at risk, they're the ones with all the options, and they're the ones with all the leverage. For every *businessperson* willing to fork out millions of dollars, there are *thousands* of talented singers. And because of the laws of supply and demand, most of the power goes to the business, not the artist. It's the business that makes the big bucks, because without the business, the artist has no visibility or fans. And that's not just in showbiz; it's a life thing. Most societies disproportionately reward risk-takers.

If an artist wanted to build their own brand without making a bad business deal or giving up the lion's share of the profits, what should they do?

They should *charge* for their brand as they *build* their brand.

The Multimillion-Dollar Cycle

Let's revisit Ariana Grande's success. Ariana charges retailers like Starbucks, Coach, and T-Mobile a hefty $800,000 to $1.6 million per sponsored Instagram post for the use of her image and brand.[17, 18] That's a substantial payday, but companies do so with little reservation because Grande's popularity drives consumer behavior enough to make that a worthwhile transaction. Her face is a magnet for attention.

Grande's influence is not just limited to the music industry. At the time of this writing, Grande is Spotify's most-followed female artist, YouTube's female artist with the most subscribers, one of *Time* magazine's most influential people in the world, and, as of 2019, the most-followed woman on Instagram. Today, she has over 350 million followers.[19] Companies recognize the potential of tapping into this vast fan base to promote their products, leveraging Grande's image of fame, fortune, glamour, and beauty. This symbiotic relationship with advertisers allows Grande to further expand her fan base, creating a cycle of mutual benefit.

By charging clothing manufacturers millions of dollars for her fashion endorsements, Grande can use that money to fund her music career. She can invest in buying new lyrics, creating better music videos, and paying for the advertising she needs to stay relevant. Her success has also allowed her to invest in her personal product lines, including a highly successful perfume company that grossed over $1 billion in sales in 2022. All this helps her expand her brand and increase her popularity, which in turn allows her to charge even more for the next set of brand deals she enters into. It creates a profitable cycle that looks like this:

EARN $$$
FROM BRAND
DEALS

RAISE FEES
FOR SUBSEQUENT
BRAND DEALS

LAUNCH
TOP 40
SONGS

REINVEST
IN EXPANDING
THE BRAND
& EMPIRE

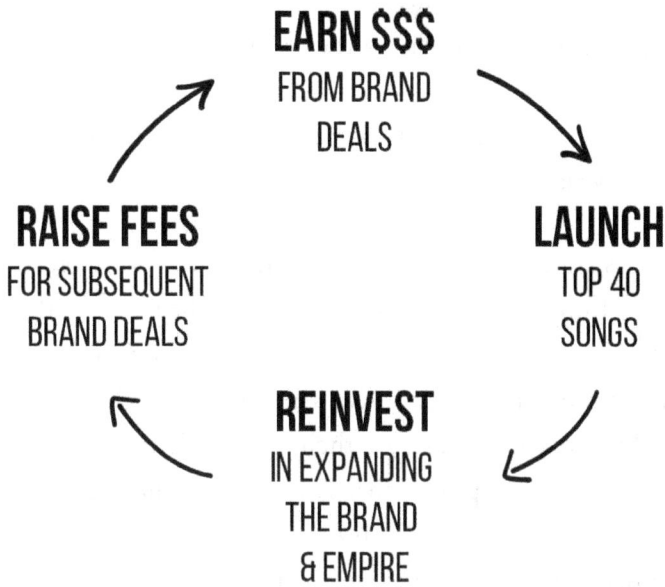

This is the value of building a strong personal brand—in any business.

In my mind, the way celebrities like Ariana Grande leverage their brand falls into two categories: leveraging fame to sell their products, and leveraging fame to sell someone else's products. Even though Ariana Grande makes a larger percentage of profit on her personal brands, her highest leverage activities are actually using her brand to sell someone else's products because she doesn't have to do any of the work. She doesn't have to worry about the product, order fulfillment, customer support, and other middlemen. All she does is smile for the camera and collect the check. Now that's true leverage! You know you've made it when you can make millions based on who you are, not what you do.

At this point, it's important to acknowledge the fragile nature of fame; Grande's career, like any celebrity's, is not immune to uncertainty. There's always the possibility that she could release a lousy record, retire early, or lose popularity. But even if Grande were to fade from the limelight, the business world would barely notice as it moved on to the next big name, leaving Grande with the wealth she accumulated during her peak.

Some critics argue that the focus on branding and commercial success takes away from the true artistry of music. They believe that music should be about creativity, emotion, and expression, not profit. And yet, *many* famous musicians adopt the same strategies as Grande to successfully grow (and sustain) their careers. That's because artists have to pay for the exposure that is required to have a career in the first place. If these artists hadn't used their brand to build their brand, these critics wouldn't be criticizing them—because they wouldn't know who they are.

Even artists who gain fame organically on platforms like YouTube still invest a significant amount of time and effort to achieve their success. What appears to be effortless fame actually required countless hours of content creation, editing, and promotion. And for every artist who does make it big, there are thousands whose efforts go unnoticed. Moreover, the few who do achieve fame organically often find that they must employ traditional marketing methods to sustain their success. These strategies help them maintain visibility, connect with a broader audience, and ultimately build a lasting brand. In this way, even seemingly *overnight* successes reveal an underlying truth: Lasting success requires deliberate and strategic brand-building efforts that require significant financial investments.

As a creator of any nature, you will always be at the mercy of the promoter or business that can get you exposure—unless you're willing and able to pay to build your brand yourself. You want to be in control of the leverage, so you can hire promoters to execute your vision instead of relying on bad business deals to make things happen. Building a successful brand takes a significant investment of time, effort, and money, but it *needs to be done*. Unless you're extremely lucky, you'll need millions of dollars to build a strong brand. So you have to find a way to make the math work in your favor. You must find ways to charge for the brand you currently have so you can scale your brand in a way that allows you to control the leverage. Bet on yourself, and charge for your brand to build your brand.

An Update on Brand-Building 101

Now that you understand the basics of the fifth law of leverage, it's time to build on that foundation. To truly succeed with this law, you will need to master the fundamentals and go way beyond them.

Start with verbalizing your value proposition: Why should someone choose your product or service over all the other options? What tangible value do you provide? What problems does your service solve? If you can't answer these questions succinctly, it will be tough to market at scale. Remember, your buyers won't buy a product they don't understand. In fact, they won't even buy a product unless they're completely convinced it will deliver significantly more value than the price they'd pay for it. So, your offer needs to be incredibly compelling.

The next step is establishing credibility. For most businesses, this means earning hundreds, if not thousands, of raving online reviews. This is a ton of work, but it's one of the highest leverage activities you'll do because positive reviews improve conversion rates long after you do the work to obtain them. Whether it's through testimonials or thought leadership pieces you create, make sure people know your brand can be trusted. You can do this through storytelling on podcasts and social media and proactively stacking up positive customer reviews. Make sure you consistently accumulate testimonials and reviews from your customers as you work with them. Remember, your favorite customers won't automatically leave you positive feedback online, so it's your job to make it easy for them to share their experiences with the world. This is hard work. A lot of times, it's more work than the actual service you're providing, but it's the work that will do the most in helping you consistently acquire customers and generate revenue. Remember, buyers pay more for brands they trust. That trust is what you're cultivating.

As you transform your image into a name people trust and prefer, it's important to not lose sight of the long-term play. Remember, this is only half the battle. You still need to crack the second part of the equation, Arianna Grande-style. It's time to charge for the brand you have so you can scale it to the next level. Luckily, there's a blueprint for this.

Learning From the Best

Since we're talking about the music industry, another artist has recently demonstrated how to regain leverage and control. Taylor Swift re-recorded her old classics to get her brand back, and I think more and more music artists will be exploring new ways to "buy back" their own success. Taylor's decision to re-record her albums stemmed from a dispute over the ownership of her master recordings. By re-recording her old hits, she not only regained control over her music but also revitalized her brand, offering fans new versions while maintaining the integrity and appeal of the originals. This move underscored her artistic independence and set a precedent for artists seeking to reclaim their work and regain the leverage they need to continue expanding their reach.

Similarly, Rihanna does a great job charging for her brand to build her brand. Much like Ariana Grande, her talents aren't restricted to performing music. Yes, she's an extraordinary singer and has sold more than 250 million records to date, but I'd argue she's successful because she's an even better dealmaker. Her wealth has been reinvested into her brand, allowing her to expand her empire beyond music into fashion and beauty, with a similar profit cycle as Ariana Grande's. Rihanna's powerful brand made her the face of Fenty, and in return, Fenty has made her a billionaire.

Rihanna doesn't manufacture Fenty products herself. Fenty was created through a collaboration with LVMH (the parent company of Louis Vuitton), which handles the production and distribution. This partnership allows Rihanna to leverage LVMH's extensive distribution channels, and they in turn leverage Rihanna as the face of their brand, driving their success.[20] This strategic partnership has made Rihanna the richest female music artist in the world. As of 2023, her net worth is $1.7 billion,[21] exactly double that of Madonna's. This demonstrates how charging for your brand can elevate it to unprecedented heights.

If you're looking for someone who's taken a different approach to applying Law Five, consider Robert Kiyosaki. He's the author of *Rich Dad, Poor Dad*, and he's used this concept to build his $100 million net worth.

Kiyosaki's businesses focus on financial education and literacy, offering books, courses, and seminars to help people achieve financial independence. While he's not the only educator with a passion for finance, his unique approach to monetizing his brand has allowed him to remain in the public spotlight for decades.

Kiyosaki has spent a great deal of time and money selling books and using the opt-in pages in the books, along with other lead magnets, to build a mailing list of over 100 million high-intent subscribers worldwide. He uses this list to promote thousands of investment-related companies, each of which pays him a percentage of the sales generated by his promotions.

Here's what Kiyosaki's profit cycle looks like:

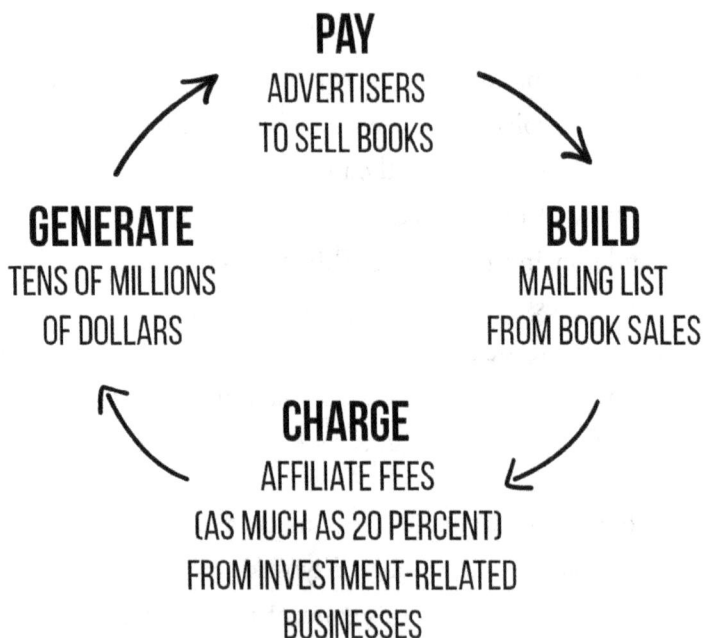

PAY
ADVERTISERS
TO SELL BOOKS

GENERATE
TENS OF MILLIONS
OF DOLLARS

BUILD
MAILING LIST
FROM BOOK SALES

CHARGE
AFFILIATE FEES
(AS MUCH AS 20 PERCENT)
FROM INVESTMENT-RELATED
BUSINESSES

Businesses are considered healthy when they maintain a 7 to 10 percent profit margin, but he charges 20 percent just for introducing companies to the marketplace. He doesn't have to deal with any manufacturing, product fulfillment, or customer complaints. All he does is make an introduction and collect his fee.

The long-term impact of charging for your brand is crucial for building and expanding it at this level. By monetizing your brand, you create opportunities to reinvest and elevate its status and reach. This principle has been a cornerstone for many successful entrepreneurs and public figures.

Take Martha Stewart, for example. Stewart established a brand so rock-solid that it was able to weather many of her public indiscretions. She built it by monetizing her expertise every step of the way through a wide range of home and garden products, books, and TV shows. This enabled her to continuously expand her market reach while maintaining high standards of quality and authenticity. The revenue from these ventures provided the necessary capital to grow her brand further.

Tony Robbins built his brand in a similar way. By charging premium fees, he has been able to fund the expansion of his brand and transform millions of lives. The capital generated from monetizing his brand allowed him to further invest in his seminars, books, and personal coaching, increasing his reach and impact.

Kylie Jenner's brand emerged with her makeup line, Kylie Cosmetics. She turned her brand into a billion-dollar empire by leveraging her social media presence. The profits from her brand enabled her to continually innovate and expand her product line, solidifying her position in the market.

UFC fighter Conor McGregor endorses Monster Energy and Reebok and reinvests the proceeds into marketing his own brands and fights. While the UFC handles the official promotion of the fights, McGregor doesn't leave success to chance and uses his own financial resources and social media platforms to increase the visibility of his events. His investment in self-promotion contributes significantly to the financial success of his fights, often resulting in record-breaking pay-per-view sales. These strategic endorsements increase his visibility and provide the capital to build his various ventures, demonstrating the power of monetizing his personal brand to further expand it.

LeBron James follows a similar path with endorsements from Coca-Cola and Nike. He funnels the millions he earns from these deals back into his athletic brands and philanthropy, reinforcing his status as a global icon. The capital from these endorsements allows him to invest in his brand and expand his influence.

These celebrities understand the power of being their own brand, charging for it, and using the profits to fund their future endeavors. By leveraging their unique gifts and structuring deals where they own equity, these individuals enjoy a freedom most people can't imagine.

So take Law Five to heart.

Be the brand.

Invest and reinvest by charging for it.

Build a super profitable business that your family can own for generations.

This is not just about making money; it's about creating a lasting legacy. By monetizing your brand, you validate its worth and pave the way for exponential growth and sustained success. The more you charge for your brand, the more resources you will have to expand, innovate, and dominate your industry.

Reality Check:

Don't wait!

Law Five comes with a difficult-to-avoid pitfall: It's easy to think, This rule isn't for me. Many people believe that charging for your brand is something only big companies can do. It's easy to put it off until you're "bigger" in the industry—which means you'll put it off and put it off indefinitely. It's time to break the cycle. Stop waiting, and start charging for the brand you already have.

In fact, the smaller your business, the more important it is to charge for it. If you are an employee, your brand may be you (and your reputation). Charge for your reputation and any goodwill you have accumulated by referring your customers to other companies. Share your buyers with people you trust, and collect referral fees and affiliate commissions. Now you have the income to invest in building something big.

Here are some practical steps to get you started: Identify potential partners with companies and individuals who offer complementary products or services to your own but are not direct competitors.

This will ensure that both parties benefit from the partnership without cannibalizing each other's market share.

Many companies offer affiliate programs, but if they don't, or if you're working with a sole proprietor, you should negotiate and establish a clear agreement. A typical affiliate partnership is 10 to 20 percent of closed revenue. Discuss commission rates, the duration for which a referral is tracked, and payment methods. Make sure the terms are mutually beneficial. Once you have agreed on the terms, set up tracking and payment systems. This usually involves providing unique affiliate links or codes to your affiliates if you're referring people with digital links. Make sure you have a reliable system for tracking sales and accurately calculating commissions.

Personal referrals to sales reps can usually be made verbally with little to no paperwork. Simply ask them to pay you on each closed sale.

By establishing affiliate partnerships, you benefit your customers and other businesses while building a revenue stream that can generate income independent of your day-to-day efforts. Separating your results from your activities is a powerful lever that can propel you forward. Embrace the potential and the opportunities.

Don't wait for the perfect time. Make now the perfect time.

Leveraged Action Steps

If you have a brand or want to build one, how can you charge to expand it further?

	Leveraged Action Steps	Your Notes
#1	**Review Hacking:** Increase positive feedback by making it easy for satisfied customers to promote your services online.	
#2	**Affiliate Marketing:** Identify additional services your customers need in addition to what you offer. Partner with these companies and earn affiliate income by referring your clients to them.	
#3	**Referral Program:** Simplify the process for your loyal customers to earn money by referring their friends to you.	

#4	**Licensing Deals:**	
	License your brand name, logo, or intellectual property to other businesses for use in their products or marketing materials.	

Chapter Five Takeaway

LAW FIVE

CHARGE FOR YOUR BRAND TO BUILD IT FURTHER.

A SIMPLE WAY YOU CAN MAKE A BIG IMPACT

Throughout this book, we've explored the power of leverage—how small actions can produce massive results. My hope is that you've already found massive value in these pages with the tools and strategies you need to achieve exponential results in your life. Now I'm asking you to take 60 seconds to leverage your thoughts to help others learn how to build wealth for their families and communities.

Imagine a person, much like yourself—dreaming of financial freedom, searching for answers, but feeling hopelessly stuck in their difficult circumstances. They want to make a change in their lives but they don't know where to look.

You could be the reason they find *The 18 Laws of Leverage*.

By sharing your thoughts in a review for this book, you have the power to help someone else discover the laws of leverage that could radically change their lives forever.

In fact, each new review for this book helps it reach hundreds of additional people—people who, just like you, are looking for answers, guidance, and the tools to unlock their full potential. And when those people have access to these ideas, more of them will find the wealth, freedom, and opportunity they need to improve their lives, which in turn improves the world around them.

So, if you've found massive value in these pages, here's how you can help:

- If you're reading this on Kindle or any e-reader, scroll to the end and share one of your big takeaways from this book.

- If you're listening to this on Audible, tap the three dots in the top right corner and select "Rate & Review."

- Or simply visit the platform where you purchased this book to share your feedback.

Your simple act of leaving a review will make a massive difference in the lives of hundreds of people. Thank you for taking this small step to help them take a chance on this book and unlock leverage in their lives.

Your biggest fan,

P.S. If you know someone who would benefit from these principles, please share this book with them. Together, we can help more people create lives of abundance and endless possibility.

Buy the Victory

"The greatest victory is that
which requires no battle."

—Sun Tzu (acclaimed Chinese military
general, writer, and philosopher)

Let's rewind to 1888, the pinnacle of America's industrial age. The rate of industrial expansion was unprecedented for its time. As new technologies were adopted to increase production capacity, new factories appeared on the horizon almost daily. The economy was booming! It was a once-in-a-lifetime chance for risk-takers and capitalists alike to amass unimaginable wealth. One such person was a Scottish-born businessman who had been investing in the American steel industry for nearly fifteen years: Andrew Carnegie.

Carnegie believed in rapid expansion, and he had both the resources and the risk appetite to support his vision. He had bought an entity called the Edgar Thomson Steel Works in Pennsylvania and, subsequently, the Keystone Bridge Company, which would eventually become the first steel plant under the banner of Carnegie Steel. By the late 1880s,

Carnegie had become one of the nation's leading steelmakers. His bold and strategic acquisitions built a vast empire of steel mills, propelling him to the forefront of the industry and establishing him as a key figure in America's industrial growth.

While Carnegie was expanding his business, another company called Homestead Steel Works had grown into a formidable competitor. Known for their skilled workforce and cutting-edge technology, Homestead also had what Carnegie envisioned as the next frontier for his empire: a vast fleet of steamships and hundreds of miles of private railroad. In 1888, Carnegie Steel acquired Homestead Works. The resulting venture, Carnegie Railways, supplied steel to cities on the Eastern Seaboard, while its barges delivered steel to the booming West via the Mississippi River.[22]

This purchase will be remembered as a significant example of a company *buying the victory*. Carnegie wanted to grow faster than everyone else in his field, so rather than enduring the slow growth and lengthy timeline required to build the infrastructure, he bought a company that already had it. This purchase shortened his path to victory and allowed him to maintain the momentum needed to finish his mission.

By the time the United States became the world's largest steel producer, Carnegie had firmly established his dominance, owning a quarter of the global market. In 1901, he sold Carnegie Steel to J.P. Morgan for $480 million, making him one of the richest men in America. Adjusting for inflation, $480 million in 1901 is approximately $16.3 billion in today's dollars (2024).

Businesses tend to default to slow and methodical growth during times of success, but Carnegie chose a different path; he mastered the art of *paying* for his wins many times over. He'd proven that buying one's victory can be a massive competitive advantage for accumulating wealth, and that's why it's an important law of leverage.

Win Without the Battle

There's a lot to learn from the famous Chinese military strategist Sun Tzu when it comes to business and wealth creation.

For all of his advice on fighting and winning wars, Sun Tzu emphasized that it was best to avoid a war in the first place. "To win one hundred victories in one hundred battles is not the acme of skill. To subdue the enemy without fighting is the acme of skill," he said.

Imagine the potential. If you could train yourself to reach your goals and win your wars without the battle, wouldn't you consider it a much better form of victory? You would circumvent many obstacles without directly overcoming them. And you would conserve your energy and time to invest elsewhere. Do you see how the various laws of leverage also tend to lean on each other? Following one law allows you the chance to implement other laws.

That's precisely what this law of leverage helps achieve: It enables you to win without a battle. Sure, "buying the win" requires foresight, courage, and capital, but it mitigates the potential for a costly defeat.

The Microsoft Way

Carnegie is hardly alone in his relentless pursuit of operational expansion. Large companies become almost unstoppable when they can afford to acquire the talent and inventions they need, and they do so by buying the victory.

Nimble startups have an insatiable desire to win, and large companies have a way of getting stuck and becoming increasingly less effective as they grow in size. This is because as a company grows in size, so does its bureaucracy. Unless addressed carefully, organizations inevitably start taking on "dead weight," that is, unmotivated hires who are more concerned with protecting the company they already have than they are with exponential growth.

When large companies do bring home a win, they do so by battling the sluggishness that frequents massive companies. Those that continue to thrive long after losing the original traits—whether people or inventions that initially made them successful—often do so by buying their next victory.

Let's take the case of Microsoft. Microsoft was the gold standard for computer software in its heyday, and it held that position for decades, largely because of the leadership of Bill Gates. However, it ran out of steam after Gates stepped back from the primary lead role to focus on other projects, a transition that posed significant challenges for the company.

But make no mistake—Microsoft remained profitable. They pivoted. They began using their war chest of resources to acquire other companies that would allow them to remain competitive. And like Carnegie Steel, their acquisitions weren't one-offs; Microsoft is what it is today because of a long series of successful wins paid for repeatedly at the opportune time.

In 2014, Microsoft bought Mojang Studios for $2.5 billion, gaining the Minecraft franchise and community to boost Xbox's appeal.

In 2016, Microsoft expanded its reach in professional networking by acquiring LinkedIn for $26 billion, gaining access to LinkedIn's 700 million-plus members. This integration led to services like LinkedIn Learning and Dynamics 365 Sales.

In 2018, Microsoft acquired GitHub for $7.5 billion to enhance its cloud offerings and developer tools, integrating GitHub's platform with Azure.

In 2021, Microsoft acquired Nuance Communications for $19.7 billion to strengthen its healthcare AI capabilities and eventually invested $10 billion in OpenAI, the company behind ChatGPT, securing future AI advancements.

These acquisitions are just a few of the two hundred-plus companies Microsoft strategically purchased to enhance its market position.[23]

Smart Companies "Buy" Customers (And so Can You)

You don't need to be a Fortune 500 CEO to apply this law. I was sitting in on a meeting recently with a twenty-six-year-old tech executive, and at one point in the meeting, he casually told the marketing director to, "Buy us an extra thousand clients for Q2." Although I'd sat in on many similar conversations, I found the way he phrased client acquisition enlightening. There was no *hope* in that statement. He wasn't *hoping* to do the work to *potentially* get another

1,000 customers. He was *paying* for the marketing machine to pump out another 1,000 customers—he was paying for a surefire win.

And I've done the same.

I bought the win with my first book, *Crush Your Kryptonite*. I calculated that it would cost around $12K to $15K in ads to keep it a number-one bestseller on Amazon.com for 100 days. I then sat down to find ways to monetize the book, in addition to the book royalties, through business consulting fees and other services on the back end of the book. Once I had a plan I felt confident would generate at least $70K in revenue on the back end, I bought the victory for $15K and collected my earnings. Instead of working for an hourly wage to generate $55K, I worked on the systems to buy the victory in a way that wasn't as dependent on my time.

After it was number one for 100 days consecutively, I moved on to the next step in that strategy, which was to maximize the LTV (lifetime value) of the customers I was bringing in from the book so I could afford the ads to sell more books. The longer I marketed *Crush Your Kryptonite*, the more I had to pay to outbid similar authors wanting a piece of the action. The reason I was able to continuously outbid the competition was that I had a higher LTV for the book. The concept is straightforward:

Step 1: Buy the victory.

Step 2: Increase the LTV (lifetime value) of the customer.

Step 3: Use your profit to continue outbidding your competition for exposure.

Buying the victory was not a one-time strategy with *Crush Your Kryptonite*. I have consistently applied this principle, and I am committed to exploring new opportunities to implement it as my business continues to grow.

Hope is a terrible marketing strategy. In general, hope is a lousy strategy, period. It's for dreamers. And while dreamers might have great ideas, it takes an action to turn dreams into reality.

You want to get yourself to the place where you know you're going to win—and in many cases, you can get there by buying the victory.

Many of the top marketers in the world aren't that great at running ads or split testing to maximize results. Instead, these top marketers just figured out how to maximize the LTV of the customer so they can afford to outbid their competitor's marketing dollars. They've figured out that buying the win is the easiest way to dominate a competitive market.

Let me explain. If your goal is to increase revenue by $100K a month, you could buy the victory by increasing the number of purchases your current clients make. If your average customer spends $4,300 with you, find ways to increase their spending to $4,800. That additional $500 of revenue multiplied by your entire client base is substantial revenue you can use to advertise and buy the victory. The key is to immediately leverage that revenue to buy more clients. That's the secret to keeping the revenue stream strong.

This principle can be applied to hiring and outsourcing as well. Let's say you have a problem in your business. Your first instinct might be to let your current employees handle it. If they lack the necessary skills, you may consider investing in their training and development, but this approach can be costly in both time and lost revenue. Depending on the problem, your reputation may even begin to suffer in the process, resulting in a smudge on your brand. Hiring someone from the outside to solve it at the highest level might make you more money than you would save by letting your current employees try their best.

There are also instances, however, when time is not a constraint, and it makes sense to train yourself or an employee in advance on a particular skill set. This is where thinking ahead pays off. By studying companies that are a few steps ahead of you, you can anticipate the challenges they faced and prepare for similar obstacles. Instead of becoming complacent during a period of growth, you can proactively invest in the necessary training or information to handle these challenges yourself. In doing so, you're leveraging the expertise of a master to save money in future endeavors.

Whether you're a budding entrepreneur or an established executive, there's no shortage of creative opportunities to buy the victory. The earlier examples for applying this law were through acquiring complementary businesses for talent, technology, or production, but you could go about it in a completely different way. You could pay for research or innovation that someone has already created for tools you need and pay them to train your team. You could buy a win with better lead generation or customer service. Or, you could form alliances with other corporations that are growing in alignment with your vision. There are lots of applications for buying the victory. Now it's up to you to find the opportunities and implement them.

Reality Check:

How often do you fight for victories you could have bought for less?

If you don't own a massive business, apply this principle on a smaller scale.

It's easy to think small when your budget is small, but what if you outsourced your challenges on a job by job basis? Many W2 employees will jump at the opportunity for side gigs, so this could be a way for you to benefit from the most skilled workers without having to hire them full time. This strategic move could lead to significant growth and success for your business, as you won't spend forever solving your challenges, or worse, resign from solving them at all.

Courses can be a beneficial way to fill knowledge gaps when time is on your side, but you may consider the cost-effectiveness of hiring someone who already has the necessary expertise to fix the issue when your back is against the wall. This way, you can quickly resolve the problem, improve your business, and learn how to prevent similar issues in the future.

This doesn't just apply to broken machinery. If you see a drop in people coming to your business, buy your way out of it. Look for experts who can update your sales and marketing processes.

Try it out—now. Speed is everything in business. The quicker you adapt to new challenges and find efficient solutions, the faster you'll be able to propel your business forward.

Leveraged Action Steps

Your turn! How can you best apply this law and *buy the victory*?

List the top example that comes to mind and go buy yourself a victory.

Your Notes

Chapter Six Takeaway

LAW SIX
Don't leave your success up to chance. Buy the victory and pay for a guaranteed result.

Focus on the Profits

"Revenue is vanity, profit is sanity, and cash is king."

—Unknown

Imagine a small bakery in your neighborhood that makes delicious pastries everyone loves. Business is good, and the bakery owner decides it's time to reinvest in the business to grow further.

But instead of opening new locations or improving the quality of their products and customer experience—actions that directly drive revenue—the owner begins spending on extravagant items. They redecorate the seating area, add expensive artwork, and make complicated, high-end desserts that look beautiful but don't appeal to the local customers. Sales rise slightly with the introduction of these fancy desserts, but expenses skyrocket because of the high cost of ingredients and decor. The once healthy profit margin starts to shrink.

Despite the rising expenses, the owner remains optimistic, believing that these investments will eventually pay off. However, as sales fluctuate, the high costs remain constant. The bakery's profits continue to decline, and the financial strain becomes more evident. This situation is not sustainable, and the owner's optimism wanes. "One day, the profits will come," insists the owner. But in many cases, they never do, leading to the business's downfall.

I've seen it happen far too often in business, and it's incredibly discouraging. Profit is not just a business's bread and butter; it's its lifeblood. It feeds the company and supports those it employs. Even if a company is currently fueled by borrowed money, someday, it will have to stand on its own two feet with its own profits.

The healthiest businesses are profitable from day one. That's the seventh law of leverage to build sustainable wealth and success: Focus on the profits.

The Pitfalls of Chasing Growth Over Profit

On a more personal note, I know an aspiring entrepreneur with a fantastic tech invention. We'll call him Ted, for now. He was onto something big. Imagine a platform that can intertwine the best capabilities of Slack, Zapier, Stripe, and Salesforce into one user-friendly, accessible package—that's what Ted was building.

His product could simplify small business interactions and transactions by using RFID business cards. (RFID business cards allow seamless sharing of contact information through a simple phone scan—a technology that's already fairly common.) Ted's creation took this feature to the next level; his platform allowed small businesses to integrate communication with their teams and customers, their payment processors, and any additional software they used without being burdened by the financial weight of tools utilized by their larger counterparts. I'm veiling the specifics to protect Ted's intellectual property, but I can confidently say that his concept had the potential to be revolutionary.

Amazing, right?

The problem with Ted's blueprint was that his passion for technology was greater than his dedication to profits. When prodded about revenue generation, he would invariably sidestep the questions to discuss the latest flashy feature in the pipeline.

Month after month, his focus remained unwaveringly anchored to the technology he was developing—while turning a profit, the very lifeblood of his entrepreneurial venture, was relegated to the shadows.

Herein lies a pivotal lesson for all entrepreneurs. While product innovation is paramount, the lifeline of any business is, and will always be, its profitability.

Profitability—not cutting-edge technology, mind-blowing design, or lightning-quick growth—safeguards you, your family, your team, your investors, and the business itself. Without profitability, the business will teeter on a precarious ledge, no matter how innovative. A fortified war chest of profits stacked up over time will equip a company with the formidable ability to navigate tough times, giving you opportunities to conjure solutions to problems that would have otherwise spelled your doom.

Nine out of every ten startups fail. And 42 percent of the ones that fail do so for one main reason: there was no market need for the product it offered.[24] Too many entrepreneurs create products before finding ways to monetize them. Law Seven, Focus on the Profits, flips this approach on its head: Why not search for a profitable business model *before* iterating on your product? Why not find a challenge people will pay to solve first, and *then* create the solution? If you hold your ideas loosely, watch your audience, study your profit, and let the market determine your moves, you'll help far more people and be much more likely to build one of the one-in-ten startups that thrive.

Let me reiterate: Profit is not just a number on a balance sheet. It's how you reward your stakeholders—your employees, vendors, and shareholders. It's how you attract more investors and sustain the expansion of your mission. It's how you maintain buffers to manage unexpected challenges. It's how you innovate and create something worth offering. Profit is how you build a stable financial foundation so your business doesn't crumble. Profit is how you reward *yourself* for your hard work and dedication.

And ultimately, profit is how you make the world a better place and maximize the number of people you can help with your offering.

Parkinson's Law of Money

Parkinson's Law of Money, also called "lifestyle creep," states that our expenses will always rise to meet our income. No matter how much we earn, our default is to spend every penny and stretch to spend a little more. This simple observation of human spending patterns carries profound implications for wealth accumulation.

When you're earning $40K a year, it's easy to assume you'll save more when your income increases tenfold, but the lifestyle creep can consume any amount of additional earnings. Your home can always be bigger, and your car can always be fancier. Even if we don't want to increase our spending, it just kind of happens sometimes.

Many of us insist this won't happen to us because we don't desire sports cars or Rolexes. However, lifestyle creep isn't always about luxury items. When we have plenty, we tend to loosen up the purse strings and finally take those dream vacations we've wanted. We'll buy higher quality food rather than the budget items. We might adopt a pet, incurring new costs for its care and maintenance. These are all positive changes, but they represent the subtle ways lifestyle creep affects everyone, regardless of their spending preferences.

The danger of succumbing to Parkinson's Law of Money is that it subtly erodes your leverage in wealth accumulation. Every dollar spent that you could have invested leaves you with less capital to leverage getting to the next level. Guard that money and invest it on more useful things like buying other people's time, buying the victory, and building your brand.

Focus on the profits, and pay yourself first.

Pay Yourself First

Even if you make an average income, the proper use of Law Seven offers you a guaranteed way to become wealthy. *Focusing on the profits* when applied to your personal finances could mean, for example, living on half of what you make, after taxes. The wealthiest people I know have made this a practice. It's easy to think that the only reason wealthy people can live off half of what they make is that they make a *lot,* but the part you don't see is that most of them started this practice long before they became wealthy. In fact, it's one of the reasons *why* they became wealthy.

If half of your current income isn't enough to support you immediately, even if you minimize your expenses, try to get there quickly. The first step is to raise your primary income. Start paying yourself first—with however much you can realistically set aside. Use that capital as leverage for Law Three (Use Other People's Time), or buy assets with the capital (which we will discuss later in Law Thirteen: Buy Assets; Limit Liabilities). Slowly, over time, aim to get to the stage where you can pay yourself first *and* live on less than half of what you make.

Make it a habit to live on half of what you earn, and it will reward you well in time. By following this practice, you'll eventually reach a point where you're making five to ten times your current income. By then, you'll have built the financial freedom to truly enjoy life, all while continuing to invest more and more, even as your spending naturally increases.

Reality Check

Are you waiting to take a profit?

I want to give you a whole new perspective on profit. While you may currently think in terms of "income minus expenses = profit," I encourage you to flip this formula on its head and think in terms of "income minus profits = expenses."

What if, for a short time, you took your profits first, no matter what, and then used the rest to cover your expenses?

Even taking a small percentage, such as 5 percent, can make a significant difference. If you're already paying yourself first, what if you increased the amount you paid yourself, just a little?

Give it a try. You have little to lose and everything to gain! Adopting this strategy can be the turning point that propels you toward exponential wealth.

Remember, the key to financial freedom is less dependent on how much you make but on how effectively you keep and multiply what you make. Make this a core practice in your financial strategy, and watch your wealth grow.

Here's my final tip on paying yourself first: If you're a W2 or 1099 employee, ask your HR department to split your paycheck into multiple accounts. Most companies offer this option. Diverting as little as 3 percent into a trading or real estate account is a way to pay yourself first that will pay you massive dividends down the line.

Leveraged Action Steps

Law Seven is simple: Bank your profits first—in business and in life.

		Leveraged Action Steps	Your Notes
#1		**Prioritize Profit:** If you own a business, how can you prioritize profit?	
#2		**Implement Profit Withdrawal:** What mechanism can you put in place to withdraw profits first as sales are made?	
#3		**Allocate Personal Finances:** For personal finances, what percentage of your check can you pay yourself *before* you pay your expenses?	
#4		**Self-Pay Automation:** Take the necessary steps to automate paying yourself first.	

Chapter Seven Takeaway

Think More Than You Work

"Thinking is the hardest work there is, which is
the probable reason why so few engage in it."

—Henry Ford (American industrialist and
founder of the Ford Motor Company)

I want to share a story with you. My friend John has always taken pride in his work ethic. At a young age, he absorbed the belief that hard work was his golden ticket to success. So, he relentlessly poured his energy into his career, day in and day out. Fresh out of college, he landed a stable job and steadily climbed the corporate ladder, staying with the same company throughout his career.

His job title became fancier, and his paycheck covered all the bills. He took on extra tasks, always went above and beyond, and took any overtime that was offered to him. He was the perfect employee. But deep down, John was beginning to realize an unsettling truth—he hadn't achieved the success he envisioned, the success promised by this "golden ticket" of hard work. Not only was his income lagging behind some of his peers, but a more troubling realization was looming on the horizon: he was missing out on something profoundly more important than monetary gain.

Precious moments with his family were slipping through his fingers like sand through clenched fists. The shadow of work constantly clouded his mind, making it difficult to be fully present even during his limited time with them. He missed parts of conversations as often as he missed his daughter's recitals and dates with his wife. At first, he believed that his hard work would be worth the end result, but as time went on, he began to question that belief. Observing his peers, he began to question the notion of *paying his dues*. Contrary to his belief, they balanced substantial family time with disproportionately higher incomes while working fewer hours than he did. "Unfair," he whispered. Yet, he refused to wear the victim's cloak forever. Gradually, he began to evaluate the differences between his career path and those of his friends.

His discontentment led him to ask a crucial question: "How can I do this better?"

First, he noticed that his friends weren't tied to one employer like he was. Over the years, they dared to explore different opportunities, a practice John had previously considered a sign of disloyalty.

Then he noticed another pattern—the industries his friends ended up in were different from where they started. In the past, he had mistakenly believed that changing industries was a detrimental endeavor that would result in wasted time bridging the knowledge gap. But as his friends succeeded in ways he couldn't, he painfully acknowledged that he was missing the mark. He saw the need for a paradigm shift.

He engaged his friends in candid conversations and retroactively studied successful career paths. Through his extensive research, he uncovered a profound truth: It's impossible to know everything at the beginning, so you must constantly reevaluate and adapt along the way.

It was hard to accept, but the status quo was no longer an option. The road to greatness involved calculated risks, and John had finally reached the point where he was willing to crucify his long-held beliefs. John began saying "no" to certain tasks at work in order to make time for strategic thinking. In these reclaimed moments, he explored uncharted professional territory and considered diverse paths to his goals. Most importantly, he committed substantial time to his family, fully immersing himself in their presence. The epiphany struck—"I don't need to work every second of my life to be successful."

For the first time in his life, John realized that he needed to work *less* and *think* more.

Turn Your Brain *On*

I'm sure you know plenty of people like John—perhaps you're even one of them!

Hard work is essential for success, but it has to be applied to the right activities, and that's where *thinking* comes into the equation. Too often, we get stuck in the grind, trying to work our way out of low productivity without giving our tasks the deep thought they deserve.

Let me show you what this looks like by comparing industries. The United States Bureau of Labor Statistics regularly publishes data on average wages by industry.[25] In their 2020 report, they revealed the average hourly earnings for the following occupations: agricultural workers (who may be the hardest workers on the planet) earn an average of $13.95 per hour, personal healthcare aides earn $13.59, child care workers earn $11.89, food service workers earn $11.47, and retail sales workers earn $12.63.

Contrast these figures with those in the same report that fall on the other end of the scale. Pharmacists make $61.88 per hour, marketing managers make $68.35, computer systems managers make $45.06, surgeons make $120.99, anesthesiologists top the list at $130.50 per hour, and blockchain engineers (a job that didn't exist until recently) make $84.11 per hour.[26]

The highest earners aren't even in those statistics because they are blazing their own paths away from these established positions. I know plenty of sales reps who make $150 to $250 an hour and real estate syndicators who make $1,000 to $2,000 an hour. These individuals are not just working hard; they are thinking strategically, identifying opportunities, and creating value in the marketplace.

The question is, who's working *harder*?

The income disparity between physical and mental work is stark. The way I see it, the lowest paying jobs compensate for physical work, while the highest paying jobs pay people to *think*. That's not to say that the *thinkers* don't work hard, but it does suggest that hard work alone is not enough.

That's why more than 5.4 million Uber drivers earn $10 to $20 an hour, while Travis Kalanick, Uber's founder who *thinks* for a living, has amassed billions.

One winter night in Paris in 2008, Travis and his friend Garrett, both serial startup founders, couldn't find a cab after a tech conference. That experience sparked a thought: *What if people could request rides from their phones?* Garrett, who would later co-found Uber, went home and registered the domain name UberCab.com. That's how Uber was born—one person saw a need and created a solution.[27]

Take Jeff Bezos for a second example. His net worth hovers around $130 billion. He's known for his dedication to thinking, which he considers to be a key driver of his success.[28] He believes that to create innovative solutions and thriving businesses, you must allocate more time to thinking than working. That's because working harder doesn't necessarily produce better results—it's the quality of the thinking behind your hard work that determines your results.

Many of Amazon's breakthroughs, from the Kindle e-reader to Amazon Web Services, owe their existence in part to this mindset. Bezos encourages small, agile teams that can move quickly, think creatively, and take ownership. He's built one of the world's most successful and innovative companies by prioritizing thinking and reflection in himself and his team.

As these leaders demonstrate (and as we can see in John's story), thinking is crucial to making sure you put your efforts in the right place. Part of that is working in the right industry. It's incredibly difficult to consistently increase your income if you're working in an outdated industry that isn't growing as fast as you are. It is important to find a growing industry with real potential for upward mobility. One way to identify these opportunities is to assess whether you can increase your income by at least 20 percent each year. If the industry and your employer aren't growing, your growth will be limited. In my mind, the only reason to work in an outdated industry is to innovate and create something new out of the ashes.

To maximize your earning potential as an employee, look for positions with a production or commission-based compensation structure. If your current job can't offer at least 20 percent annual income growth, it may be time to explore new options.

When Working Harder is *Not* the Solution

In a study by Mental Health America, a staggering 77 percent of respondents reported feeling completely burned out from their jobs.[29] Translated to monetary terms, the cost of this burnout and job stress (from resignations, health issues, and lost productivity) for U.S.-based businesses is $300 billion.[30] To put it in perspective, that's roughly the size of Finland's economy.[31]

Working harder with blinders on is not the answer. Overworking leads to unimpressive results. Success comes not from pushing harder and working longer hours but from thinking deeply, listening carefully, and continuously learning and growing. When people consistently grow their skills and income, they can work forever. It's when we stop growing that we experience burnout. I know many people who work sixty-plus hours a week and are happy, healthy, and excited to work on Monday, and I know people who work half that and dread the morning alarm clock. The difference is not the amount of work; it's the amount of *life* we get out of our work. That's the difference here.

Albert Einstein is renowned for his thought experiments and would allocate days to reflect deeply on specific concepts. He didn't see himself as extraordinary; he was "passionately curious." Warren

Buffett, the Oracle of Omaha, doesn't trade stocks all the time; a significant portion of his day revolves around reading and processing financial data. Bill Gates famously devoted time twice a year to his "Think Week"—a period for original, innovative thinking that shaped Microsoft's future endeavors.

Many of today's leading executives are incorporating mindfulness and other contemplative practices into their work routines. They not only practice these methods themselves but encourage their teams to do the same.

Becoming a Deliberate Thinker

Deliberate thinking isn't something you're born with; it's something you consciously cultivate. Small, deliberate acts of personal improvement compound over time. James Clear, author of *Atomic Habits*, points out that improving just 1 percent every day leads to a thirty-seven-fold improvement over the course of a year.

Let's say you work in sales. For the next quarter, you could focus on enhancing your sales pitch by 2 percent. Next, you find ways to improve your service delivery by another 2 percent. Then you could work on eliminating 20 percent of your time-wasting activities and redirecting that time into tasks that increase revenue, reduce costs, and free up even more time. With the extra time margin, you could find ways to improve your unique selling proposition and the way you position your product or service to your customers. Then you can improve your customer guarantees to give the highest percentage of your customers the confidence to choose you over the competition, shortening sales cycles and allowing you to help more people faster, which increases revenue. These improvements don't just add up; they compound, giving you exponential results.

I know salespeople who make $60K a year working seventy-hour weeks, and I know salespeople making $600K a year working forty-hour weeks. One core difference between them is that one spends all their time working, while the other spends time *working the system* and making consistent, incremental improvements.

If you want inspiration on how to apply intentional thinking to your work, look at what other companies are doing.

Google fosters creativity through its "20 percent time" policy, which encourages employees to dedicate at least 20 percent of their work time to personal projects they're passionate about. This freedom to think creatively has led to many successful projects, including Gmail, Google News, and AdSense.[32]

IDEO is a design and innovation consulting firm that thrives on brainstorming. Their "design thinking" approach emphasizes experimentation and iteration, resulting in groundbreaking solutions like the first Apple mouse, the Swiffer Sweeper, and Target's redesigned shopping cart.

Pixar, known for its animation excellence, relies on rigorous review processes in which multiple teams refine ideas before production approval. This approach has given us beloved films like *Toy Story*, *Finding Nemo*, and *The Incredibles*.

Zappos, the online fashion retailer, exemplifies commitment to continuous learning and improvement. They consistently encourage employees to reflect and think creatively about enhancing the customer experience. This deliberate practice, applied to more than 1,500 employees, has enabled Zappos to maintain a customer retention rate of over 75 percent and generate an average of approximately one billion in annual revenue over the past five years.[33]

Becoming a better thinker isn't rocket science. Sometimes it's as simple as setting aside the first few hours of your Monday just to think. The more consistently you block off distraction-free time, the better results you'll get from your deliberate thinking.

Your growth will speak for itself.

Thinking for the Long Term

After my friend John made his crucial pivot, his life took a remarkable turn. By prioritizing strategic thinking and career exploration over menial tasks, he discovered new opportunities at an emerging technology company that was happy to pay him for his output rather than the hours he put in. This transition has tripled his income over the past few years, but more importantly, it's given him the time he needs to invest in more important things.

Once he regained control of his time, John became an active participant in his family's life. He started going on regular dates with his wife, attending his daughter's recitals, and rediscovering hobbies he had previously abandoned. As a result, John is living a more fulfilling, well-rounded life that closely aligns with the success he had always envisioned.

John's journey underscores a crucial point: Those who *think* more, *grow* more. As author James Allen puts it, "You are today where your thoughts have brought you; you will be tomorrow where your thoughts take you!"

So where exactly are your thoughts taking you?

Consider this: If you continue down the same path your current thoughts are taking you, will you be satisfied with where you end up? Or do you feel the need to pause, reflect on the bigger picture, and perhaps start fresh like John did?

Having a clear vision and working steadily toward it is critical. It serves as a North Star to guide you through the darkest of times. Without adequate consideration of the big picture for your life and your work goals, and without conscious, long-term thinking, you may find yourself without direction, unable to move in harmony with your goals.

Your vision is the compass for your decisions, the driving force behind your motivation, the yardstick by which you measure your progress, the benchmark for your achievements, and the magnet that attracts like-minded people to your cause. With a well-defined vision, you'll focus on solving the right problems. You'll exhibit patience, adaptability, optimization, and resilience because you know where you're going.

By committing to long-term thinking and regularly reevaluating your path, you can achieve the success and fulfillment that comes from aligning your actions with your deepest values and aspirations.

Reality Check

Where's the bottleneck?

If you're an employee, it can be hard to know if and why your results are stagnating. Here's a simple framework to get you back on track:

The first step is to understand and verbalize the job you were hired to do. What is your employer's goal, and why are they paying you? Once you've identified the expected outcome, the next step is to identify the bottleneck that is limiting your progress toward that goal.

With this understanding, develop a concrete strategy to remove the bottleneck. The shorter the feedback loop, the faster you will innovate and the more output you will get for your input.

Implement your strategy over a designated period and reflect on the results. What worked, what didn't, and why or why not? Then identify the next bottleneck and repeat.

Commit to continually eliminating bottlenecks over the next six to twelve months. By doing so, your growth should propel you into the upper echelons of performance in your field.

Once you have increased your output, you will have even more time to think, more time with your family, more time to innovate, and more time to do the things you value most.

Think more than you work.

Leveraged Action Steps

Your turn! How can you think more than you work to get better results?

	Leveraged Action Steps	Your Notes
#1	Define the outcomes you wish to see in your life.	
#2	Create a strategy toward achieving that outcome.	
#3	Execute said strategy over a specific period of time.	
#4	Reflect on the results.	
#5	Identify the bottlenecks in your strategy and solve them.	

Chapter Eight Takeaway

LAW EIGHT
YOUR STRATEGY WILL TAKE YOU FURTHER THAN RELENTLESS HARD WORK.

Master Your Strengths; Ignore the Rest

"There's no sixteen-step formula for becoming Beyoncé."

—Gary Vaynerchuk ("Gary Vee," American entrepreneur and media influencer)

In the vast and glittering world of Hollywood, countless aspiring actors and actresses spend their lives grasping at the spotlight's warm glow. Their dreams of stardom fuel their relentless dedication to mastering their craft. Yet, for many, the path to stardom remains elusive, shrouded in uncertainty and dashed hopes. Instead of gracing the silver screen, they find themselves trapped in mundane jobs they despise, all while clinging tightly to the fantasy of fame.

Life offers us a vast array of opportunities, each with its unique blend of rewards and varying probabilities of success. The choices we make in response to these opportunities will impact where we end up. Do we devote our focus to fleeting prospects? Do we follow a conventional trajectory? Or do we grace ourselves with the humility needed to acknowledge where our gifts, talents, and strengths really are, and then channel our efforts into nurturing them?

Consider another situation, one more elusive than the first. Imagine someone who is five feet tall and devotes all of their energy to becoming a professional basketball player in the NBA—a field in which towering height is virtually a prerequisite for the job. The dream may be intoxicating, their passion undeniable, but harsh realities loom in the distance. Is it possible they might succeed? Yes, it is technically possible because it's been done before. But is it *likely?* No. It would be a career path fraught with monumental challenges and uncertainties, where even achieving mediocrity would be a distant conquest. In such a scenario, a pivotal choice arises—a crossroads where individuals must confront reality and consider alternative avenues for their unique strengths to shine.

The advice in these examples may seem obvious. The folly of pursuing a professional basketball career with a height disadvantage is self-evident, but we often overlook similar follies when making other choices in the subtle and nuanced areas of life. This law challenges us to reconsider the pivotal career choices we make without considering their long-term implications.

Every person has a mix of strengths and weaknesses, a unique pattern that sets us apart. This is the focal point of Law Nine: Master Your Strengths; Ignore the Rest. The real challenge is recognizing this mix and figuring out where to focus our efforts. It means being fully committed to developing our talents consistently and persistently, and only moving on once we've become exceptionally proficient at our natural gifts.

In navigating the labyrinth of life, it's evident that those who get the furthest are the ones who focus on developing their strengths rather than their weaknesses. As Gary Vaynerchuk said, "There's no sixteen-step formula for becoming Beyoncé." Don't waste your time striving for something you can't become. True satisfaction comes when our pursuits are in harmony with our innate talents and strengths. It's not about pursuing every opportunity that comes our way; it's about recognizing where our unique brilliance can truly shine. By making this conscious choice, we embark on the journey that is most likely to lead to extraordinary achievements and a truly satisfying life. Instead of chasing a goal we can't reach, we can sit back and enjoy the success we *can* achieve.

Strengths Versus Weaknesses

This principle may seem counterintuitive. After all, a significant portion of existing motivational content revolves around identifying and fixing our weaknesses. However, I invite you to consider an alternative perspective. Instead of allocating the bulk of your efforts on improving your weaknesses, what if you doubled down on your strengths?

I firmly believe that obsessively seeking out and eradicating our weaknesses is an inherently flawed approach to improving our abilities, because it often comes at the expense of honing our strengths. Our energy and time are finite resources, and attempting to tackle both strengths and weaknesses simultaneously can lead to the perilous precipice of burnout, a state we desperately want to avoid.

I propose you dedicate most of your time to sharpening the gifts you already possess and a limited amount of time to strengthening your weaknesses. Everyone has natural strengths, whether they are obvious or not. If you are uncertain of what your strengths are, take the time to rediscover them.

To best apply the laws of leverage, focus wholeheartedly on your strengths and talents and ignore the internal and external critics who remind you of your weaknesses.

Focus on Your Strengths Like a Billionaire

Once you've embraced the idea of maximizing your strengths and temporarily shelving your weaknesses, your actions will naturally begin to shift.

Do you remember Law Three: Use Other People's Time? Once you've identified your strengths, you'll also identify areas you can delegate and outsource to others, thus allowing you to develop your natural talents more effectively. Remember, no one exists as an island unto themselves; we all benefit from each other. It's not about accomplishing everything yourself; it's about choosing the right help from the right people at the right time.

For all his visionary genius, Steve Jobs had limited technical skills. He relied heavily on a team of brilliant engineers to bring his creative vision to life. Did that reliance diminish his legacy? Absolutely not. Success is about recognizing what you excel at—what you do better than anyone else—and then unapologetically focusing on that and relying on others to fill in the blanks.

Consider Warren Buffett, a close friend of Bill Gates. Despite Gates's persistent nudging to invest in the hottest new tech companies,

Buffett wisely refused, knowing that he wasn't particularly tech-savvy. He steadfastly avoided investing in industries he didn't understand, a decision that ultimately paid dividends. Yes, Warren missed out on the meteoric rises of several tech giants, but here's the brilliance of it: he also sidestepped significant losses. Over the years, Buffett's unwavering focus on the industries he understood paved the way for his extraordinary success. In his own words, he states, "In fifty-eight years of Berkshire management, most of my capital-allocation decisions have been no better than so-so. Our satisfactory results have been the product of about a dozen truly good decisions."

The key, then, is to cultivate the discipline to hone your talents rather than fixate on your weaknesses. Buffett's fortune was largely built on just twelve key decisions. Just twelve! That's not an extensive list by any stretch of the imagination. It's an average of one monumental decision every four and a half years. But these twelve decisions had a monumental impact because Buffett spent a lifetime honing his craft and meticulously eliminating distractions. This would not have happened if he had focused on his weaknesses.

The Power of Intention and Laser Focus

Intention is the compass that guides your actions. When you set a clear intention to hone your strengths, you set a course for success. This intention becomes your unwavering commitment to personal growth, continuous improvement, and the relentless pursuit of excellence in your chosen field.

Consider this: Elite athletes don't become champions by trying to master every sport. They don't divide their energy between swimming, basketball, and track. Instead, they choose one sport, one arena in which they excel, and dedicate their heart and soul to it. That unwavering commitment is what carries them to greatness.

Similarly, you must treat your strengths as your chosen arena. This is where you will compete, excel, and ultimately triumph. Your intention becomes the driving force behind every action you take to improve your skills, expand your knowledge, and push the boundaries of what you thought was possible in your field.

The Relentless Pursuit of Mastery

Mastery is not an overnight achievement; it's a lifelong journey. To master your strengths, you must embrace the pursuit of mastery as a way of life. This means dedicating yourself to continuous learning, growth, and refinement.

Leonardo da Vinci is one of the most iconic figures in the world of mastery. He was not only a painter but also a scientist, engineer, and inventor. His mastery knew no bounds. But what often goes unnoticed is that he never tried to master everything simultaneously. He didn't become a world-renowned painter, scientist, engineer, and inventor all at once. Instead, he focused on one discipline at a time, delving deeply into its intricacies. Only when he felt he had achieved mastery did he move on to the next.

Your journey toward mastering your strengths should mirror this approach. Embrace one strength at a time, immerse yourself in it, and relentlessly pursue mastery. Commit to becoming the best in your chosen field, and use whatever means necessary to get there—whether through deliberate practice, emulation of mentors, or self-education. And while you develop your strengths, put your weaknesses on the back burner for later. Remember, you can always *use other people's time* and skill sets for the areas you're not good at.

The Fear of Mediocrity

The fear of mediocrity is a potent force that can either drive you to greatness or paralyze you with self-doubt. At some point, you will inevitably question whether you're making the right choices or if your time would be better spent elsewhere.

It's important to remember that the pursuit of mastery is not a linear path. There will be setbacks, plateaus, and moments of uncertainty. But here's the truth: The fear of mediocrity is often a sign that you're on the right track. It shows that you're pushing yourself beyond your comfort zone in the pursuit of excellence.

When you encounter this fear, embrace it as a companion on your journey. Let it remind you that you're striving for something extraordinary. Even the most accomplished individuals experience doubt and imposter syndrome. What sets them apart is their ability to persevere and keep pursuing their strengths.

The Art of Saying No

As you commit to mastering your strengths, you'll discover that time is your most precious resource. To maximize your progress, you must become a master prioritizer and learn the art of saying no to things that do not align with your mission.

Warren Buffett is a master of saying no. Despite the countless investment opportunities that come his way, he remains disciplined in his focus. He knows that spreading himself too thin would dilute his ability to excel in his chosen field of value investing.

Similarly, you must be discerning in your choices. Evaluate every opportunity through the lens of your strengths and goals. Ask yourself if it will contribute to mastery in your chosen arena, or if it will divide your energy and attention. Learn to say no to distractions and endeavors that do not serve your greater purpose.

Looking Inward: Embracing Your Strengths

You might still be unsure about the idea of "forgetting about your weaknesses," and that's completely understandable. It's not a concept you encounter often because, quite frankly, it's an unpopular opinion.

The resistance to this idea may stem from our tendency to seek external validation for what we "should" be doing, rather than focusing on what we already excel at and could do more of. If you reflect on your wandering thoughts, you might notice that your brain will highlight areas where you fell short—in other words, your weaknesses.

For instance, if someone criticizes you, you'll dwell on it more than the ten things people praised you for. Our natural response is to overallocate our behavioral improvements on the areas we're insecure about and neglect the rest. Repeating this pattern over time modifies our behavior to fit our environment but overlooks the benefits of mastering the areas where we naturally excel.

We are inherently social creatures, and the quest for validation is integral to our biological and psychological makeup. For thousands of millennia, seeking validation from our peers was not just about feeling accepted or fitting in—it was about survival. Even today, the desire for validation is instinctual. We instinctively seek validation for our choices, words, thoughts, feelings, behaviors, and actions. We crave affirmation, feedback, camaraderie, and security.

Social unity is emphasized in nearly all cultures, much as it was in our ancestral tribes of long ago. As a result, we've grown accustomed to being part of a group and continually seek external acceptance and self-affirmation. Unfortunately, as you've likely experienced, the downside of this pattern is that it tends to place disproportionate emphasis on our weaknesses rather than our strengths.

And if that wasn't reason enough, remember that the loudest voices in your life are rarely from the ones who have your best interests in mind. Instead, these thunderous voices have their *own* interests backing their comments. Whether intentional or subconscious, people try to change *our* behavior to suit *their* needs.

Reflect on the loud and persistent voices that have advised and criticized you throughout your life. These voices can come from well-meaning friends, concerned family members, or acquaintances. Their intentions might be good, but their advice may push you toward conformity and away from your unique path.

The key question is: Do you want to live like your critics? Do you find their lives inspiring and aspirational? Even more importantly, do their paths match your goals?

Identifying voices that match your goals and life vision is essential when determining who to listen to and where to invest your valuable resources. It takes courage to distinguish external expectations from internal desires—but by doing so, you liberate yourself from external validation and the opinions of others.

Remember that your path toward greatness requires deviating from the monotoned chorus of external voices and the choices they think are wise. It requires unwavering dedication to your unique strengths, gifts, and talents.

Breaking Free from External Validation

I've spoken with many elite entrepreneurs, musicians, and athletes who seem to unanimously agree that a pivotal part of their journey to the top was pushing past the bombardment of unhelpful and unsolicited advice.

"That's a waste of time."

"Don't be a workaholic."

"You look good enough. Why are you still working out?"

You've likely encountered similar discouragements when pursuing big goals. Whether these people are telling you this to feel better about themselves or whether they're genuinely trying to help, their advice can be more destructive than it is helpful. Let these comments slide, and do not let them sway you from your course. Here's why: If your critics see you reaching for spectacular things, and their advice is some form of "Do less," "Try less," or "Play it safe," it's likely because they've experienced failure and have given up on their own dreams.

The difficult part is recognizing the difference between helpful and destructive feedback. If someone genuinely wants the best for you and encourages you to pivot so you can go further—listen. If their advice is coming from a questionable place or will lead to taking your foot off the gas pedal, you may consider ignoring it. When you have a strength you know you can master and dreams worth pursuing, don't let your inner critic or external voices deter you from pursuing them. Remember, just because your critics don't have what it takes to achieve your dreams, doesn't mean you don't.

Liberating yourself from the need for external validation is a challenging, yet profoundly transformative journey. It's a path that can only be forged from within by building your internal validation system. When you genuinely understand, embrace, and believe in your strengths, the opinions of others become less important. The way to master the ninth law of leverage is to own your unique advantage and go full steam ahead, whatever others may say.

Find a Single Strength. Focus. Execute. Repeat.

Once you wholeheartedly commit to honing your strengths, it's only a matter of time before you uncover or rediscover them. The next natural step is execution.

While self-awareness and great ideas are undoubtedly valuable, they're merely the first steps in a longer journey. The true essence of success lies in the execution of those ideas. Developing the habit of consistently doing the right things takes a lot of work. Although it's an essential prerequisite for achieving meaningful success in any aspect of life, only a select few follow through with consistent execution. Once you gain clarity on leveraging your strengths fully, your achievements will stem from persistent, disciplined action.

To surpass 99 percent of your peers, you must execute better than 99 percent of them. Knowledge is easy; turning that knowledge into massive action is the challenging part that will transform your life and make you stand out among the masses.

Reality Check

Leverage what you already know.

It's impossible to master every skill, so focus on a few of your existing strengths. Hone them into a fine, precise knife and carve out your victory.

Here are a few examples of basic skill sets at different levels of development and the results and income they produce on an annual basis.

Communication:

Talking with friends: $0

Sales: $60K to $100K

High-ticket Sales: $200K to $400K

Owning multiple businesses, hiring and leading teams to close deals for you: infinite income

Technology:

Playing with computers: $0

Coding for corporations: $90K

Inventing and selling code that solves tangible problems: infinite income

If you already have a skill, develop it to the fullest.

Even seemingly simple skills like communication can take you from making sixty grand a year, to hundreds of thousands a year, to millions if you learn to negotiate and close deals well.

Whatever your skill set is, find ways to leverage it to the fullest.

Leveraged Action Steps

The ninth law of leverage is about celebrating your genius—so it's time to assess and prioritize your strengths.

	Leveraged Action Steps	Your Notes
#1	**Strength Assessment:** Evaluate your strengths honestly. What are your natural talents?	

#2	**Clarify Your Purpose:** Define your goals and objectives. Be specific and take the time needed to articulate them fully.	
#3	**Self-Evaluation:** Are you spending the bulk of your effort developing your strengths? If not, is there anything you should stop developing?	
#4	**Execution:** Develop a plan to capitalize on your strengths. Set clear deadlines and break goals into manageable steps.	
#5	**Measure and Adapt:** Monitor progress and adjust strategy as needed. Accept that growth and development are ongoing endeavors.	

Chapter Nine Takeaway

LAW NINE

Focus on your highest leverage
skills to maximize your impact.

Conserve Your Power

"Every second is of infinite value."

—Goethe

On April 6th, 2007, a young woman fell at her work desk. She cracked her cheekbone, cut her skin right on top of her eye, and eventually passed out in a small pool of her own blood. She woke up terrified. Multiple tests were done. The results all pointed to the same explanation—exhaustion. She had pushed herself to the brink, working eighteen hours daily, building the Huffington Post.[34]

In hindsight, Arianna Huffington called this episode her "wake-up call." It forced her to change her ways, and inspired her to write the books *The Sleep Revolution* and *Thrive*.[35] This event forced her to confront the fact she had overwhelmed herself with unnecessary tasks. Not only was she suffering physical afflictions, but she was trying to manage everything herself instead of working within her scope of genius. She had to eliminate the added stress before she could do that. And so do you.

Burnout is Everywhere

Burnout takes the fun out of everything and robs us of the joy we might otherwise find in our work.

Some people argue that burnout isn't real because it hasn't been officially classified as a disease or medical condition, but it is undeniably real. The World Health Organization, in the eleventh edition of the International Classification of Diseases, recognizes burnout as an occupational phenomenon, describing it as "a syndrome conceptualized as resulting from chronic workplace stress that has not been successfully managed."[36] The WHO explains that burnout is associated with energy depletion, exhaustion, mental distancing from work, cynicism, and lost efficiency, among other adverse effects.

Most hard workers have experienced burnout at some point. A Deloitte study found that 77 percent of professionals have experienced burnout throughout their careers.[37] We're all running toward something. We push ourselves to the limit when doing what needs to be done and often forget that conserving our power for the opportune time is a strength, not a weakness.

This book is about pushing your limits and using leverage intelligently to achieve more, but Law Ten focuses on a very different aspect of leverage: conserving your power.

I'm not here to tell you to lower your goals and do less. Quite the opposite. I'm here to tell you to stop doing things that aren't your most leveraged, most important tasks.

The world is full of voices urging you to slow down and take it easy, but I've never met a multimillionaire who got there by doing the bare minimum. The real solution is not to reduce your efforts, but to eliminate the time wasters that drain your energy. Imagine channeling your conserved energy back into your highest leverage tasks, working with an intensity that produces remarkable results without the burnout. By focusing your energy on what really matters, you can achieve exponential results that make hard work feel rewarding, something you look forward to. Not only does this strategy conserve your energy, but it also amplifies your impact and transforms hard work into an enjoyable and fulfilling journey to prosperity.

I'm guessing that most people reading this book are aware of some obvious energy wasters, like the never-ending stream of social media posts, emails, and media that has been purposely designed to be addictive. Technology is supposed to help us, not hinder us—so get rid of that stuff. Your power drains could be toxic relationships—these are easy to identify but difficult to remove. The hardest power drainers to identify are the ones that masquerade as important tasks. And that's what we'll focus on here.

Distinguish Urgent from Important

Picture this: Your sales manager comes in and comments about your colleague, Dave. "You know, Dave has been crushing it lately. Remember when you used to be at the top of the leaderboard every month, just like him?" This passing remark is a classic example of being nudged toward what seems urgent but may not be important to your long-term vision.

Here's the thing: The urgent activities scream for our attention by masquerading as tasks that demand immediate action. But not everything that demands your attention is worthy of it.

The essence of conserving your power is keeping the urgent from overshadowing your most important activities. Urgent tasks are like quicksand: the more you struggle, the deeper you sink, diverting your energy from tasks that could shape your future. The trick is to identify the tasks that contribute most to your long-term goals and build your empire one brick at a time.

As we mentioned in the last chapter, start saying no more often—no to tasks that drain you without contributing to your grand vision, and no to distractions that look like opportunities. Whenever you face a task, ask yourself: "Is this building my empire, or just keeping me busy?" If it's the latter, it's time to step back and refocus.

This doesn't mean neglecting your responsibilities; it means prioritizing them to align with your ultimate goals. Save your energy for high-leverage tasks that will yield significant returns and propel you toward your desired result. Remember, every no to a low-leverage task is a yes to your empire. So if getting your name above Dave's on the leaderboard is your highest leverage task, do it. But if you already have the resources you need and can better utilize that effort elsewhere, don't let the urgent activities keep you from innovating your way to the next level.

By mastering this distinction and applying the principle of leverage, you pave the way for growth, efficiency, and ultimately, the success you seek.

Ownership Over Time

No one gets rich by renting their time to the highest bidder. It doesn't matter how much you're paid, you won't get rich trading time for dollars. Renting your time is like running on a treadmill. No matter how fast you run or how long you keep moving, the moment you stop, you fall off the treadmill—and stop getting paid. The advantage of ownership is that once you've built and nurtured your machine, you can step off the treadmill and let it pay dividends forever—it works for you, creating value and wealth even in your absence.

Ownership is the cornerstone of financial freedom. While renting your time can provide immediate gains, owning assets or business interests is what truly builds long-term wealth. There is a big difference between having a steady income and building an ever-expanding income stream that grows independently of your day-to-day efforts. Ownership allows you to harness the power of compound growth, where your assets increase in value and multiply over time.

So how do you go from trading hours for dollars to becoming an owner? Start by identifying opportunities to invest your time and resources into something you can own. I recommend starting small.

Here are a few things you can do to become an owner and build equity:

1. Join an investment club: Investment clubs are groups of individuals who pool their money to invest in real estate or other similar assets. By joining a club, you gain access to larger investment opportunities and share in the ownership and profits of the group's investments without having to buy or manage the asset yourself. (Real estate professionals are

constantly raising capital for their businesses, so this is an easy way to build equity that requires very little skill and time.)

2. Sell insurance: Get an insurance license and sell policies that pay you as long as the customers pay their premiums. This is a great way to build passive cash flow so that when you get off the treadmill, you are still receiving income from your previous efforts.

3. Buy stock: Even simple things like buying stock in the Dow Jones can help you get a tiny slice of equity.

4. Negotiate for stock options: If you're at the point in your career where you're exceptionally valuable to the marketplace, try negotiating for ownership or stock options during your next job interview. This is another way to increase your ownership and equity.

Whether it's buying stock in a company or starting a side business, the key is to get started. Even the smallest steps can lay the foundation for your transition from salary to ownership.

Focus on the Critical 1 Percent

It's a sobering realization that not all effort is created equal. Only a tiny fraction of what you do produces most of your results. This principle is observed across many fields and industries. You achieve outstanding results by identifying and focusing on that critical 1 percent without proportionately increasing your effort.

Ninety-nine percent of your effort is wasted on tasks that aren't the most important 1 percent. No matter how efficient you are, there is always a new 1 percent of your tasks that could be prioritized. The key is to identify which actions and decisions will produce the most results. Look for tasks that have a multiplier effect, creating a chain reaction of positive results. These are rarely the most obvious or urgent items, but rather the ones that require strategic insight to identify and implement.

With that said, the more you learn, the less you diversify. In a world that often celebrates the jack of all trades, it's important to recognize the power of specialized knowledge. While being well rounded has its merits, deep expertise in a single area can be far more impactful.

Expertise and diversification are at opposite ends of the spectrum. While diversification spreads your risk, expertise deepens your impact. Deep knowledge in a particular field can significantly amplify your efforts, creating opportunities and openings that broad knowledge simply cannot.

Deep knowledge in a specific area allows you to recognize opportunities that others can't, solve problems with greater innovation, and offer insights that add meaningful value. This depth can make diversification less necessary because your expertise provides a unique competitive advantage and high marketability.

By diversifying less and doing fewer things, you save your mental bandwidth for the most important tasks.

I'll use revenue generation as an example. Generating revenue can include the following activities: lead generation, sales calls, follow-ups, emails, and a plethora of busy work.

The following observations may not apply to your situation, but for my industry, following up with prospects outside of the first forty-eight hours of contact produces limited results. You need to either follow up with them quickly, or not follow up with them at all. When applied on a large scale, all our follow-ups might only convert 1 or 2 percent into sales. I could spend a week's worth of time following up with a hundred prospects five to ten times each to generate a single sale—or I could eliminate the follow-ups and spend the same time with new prospects, generating ten or twenty times the revenue. Another big time suck in the revenue generation process is responding to emails from prospects who are curious enough to ask questions but clearly have no intention of purchasing. I could respond to every single long, in-depth question, send hundreds of responses, and generate virtually no results—or I could acknowledge that this is not a top 1 percent use of time and stop catering to non-buyers.

My solution to protect my time while still honoring non-buyers is to respond with video responses or send them a fifteen-minute booking link to get back on my calendar. Very few non-prospects will book a fifteen-minute session, which saves me time—if they won't commit to fifteen minutes, they won't commit to hiring me. The ones who do book a session prove they're worth my time. This technique helps me spend the majority of my time with the right people and on the right activities.

For the vast majority of things, spending time with capable people who are able and willing to hire me is the 1 percent best use of my time.

It's Going to be Hard

I want to make one thing clear. When I say *conserve your power*, I'm not encouraging laziness. I'm not saying there's a cheat code to getting rich. What I'm advocating is saving energy to use where it counts. I hate to be the bearer of bad news, but hard work is absolutely required to develop rare and valuable skills.

The real magic happens when all your efforts are directed to areas that align with your mission. It's about choosing to work hard on the right things that will enhance your skills and position you for greater opportunities. Avoid the pitfalls of unproductive hard work by constantly evaluating the impact of your efforts and adjusting your course as needed to stay on target.

This brings us to the power of obsession. When you're building something big, obsession is one of the most helpful traits for getting you there. When aligned with your goals and passions, obsession can be a powerful engine for progress. It fuels perseverance, deepens focus, and elevates standards. One key to developing a healthy obsession to achieve your goals is to do fewer things and make room for the things that matter.

Managing your energy to sustain your obsession means recognizing when to immerse yourself in your work and when to recharge. Balancing intense periods of focus with necessary breaks to prevent burnout ensures that your obsession contributes to creation rather than depletion.

To ensure that your obsession produces productive results, set clear goals and boundaries for the tasks you will say no to in order to conserve your energy for the most important tasks. Use your obsession to drive you toward these goals, but also cultivate self-awareness to recognize when your focus becomes counterproductive.

Arianna Huffington sums it up perfectly in her book *Thrive*, where she says, "I do everything I can to make my life more convenient.

I outsource as much as I can to free up my time to focus on what's important to me." This approach isn't about reducing your overall effort, but about conserving your power by eliminating the trivial tasks that don't align with your core goals. When Huffington made healthy life changes, stopped doing unimportant work, and outsourced everything she could, her positive impact on the world increased significantly.

By making strategic choices that align with your vision, you can exponentially increase your impact and success. Apply these strategies diligently, and you'll transform not only your work but your entire approach to life.

Reality Check

What is your time actually worth?

Knowing the true value of your time is crucial for achieving extraordinary results. Here's how you can maximize your efficiency and impact:

Analyze Your Activities: Identify which small actions lead to big results and focus more on these high-impact activities.

Calculate Your Hourly Rate: Determine how much revenue each task generates. The following example will be most relevant to sales reps, entrepreneurs, and commission-based/project-based workers, but apply the concept to your specific situation.

If you were to itemize five of the top things you spend your time on, how much time you spent on them, and assign a rough estimate for the revenue each task generates for you, it might look something like this.

- Office Cleaning: thirty minutes spent generating $0/ hour.

- Prospecting: fifteen hours spent generating $25/hour.

- Cold-calling: fifteen hours spent generating $40/hour.

- Closing Deals with Scheduled Appointments: fifteen hours spent generating $150/hour.

- Mowing the Lawn: two hours spent generating $0/ hour.

Prioritize and Outsource: *Now that you've listed how much revenue each task generates, focus on the top activities that drive the most results and eliminate, outsource, or deprioritize lower value tasks. For instance:*

- Mowing the Lawn: two hours spent generating $0/ hour. (Outsource for $30/week.)

- Office Cleaning: thirty minutes spent generating $0/ hour. (Do it at the end of the day or hire a cleaner.)

- Prospecting: fifteen hours spent generating $25/hour. (Outsource for $375/week.)

- Cold-calling: fifteen hours spent generating $40/hour. (Eliminate and invest more in prospecting.)

- Closing Deals with Scheduled Appointments: (Double down on this task and spend thirty hours generating $150/hour.)

- The key leverage point here is to increase the current 15 hours of outsourced prospecting to 30 or even 300 hours, allowing you or your sales team to spend more time closing deals.

Focus on High-Leverage Tasks: Identify tasks that generate the highest hourly rate. Reduce time spent on low-leverage tasks to increase time spent on high-leverage tasks.

Establish Your Aspirational Hourly Rate: Determine a target hourly rate based on your high-value tasks. Use this rate to decide which tasks to take on. Delegate, defer, or decline tasks that don't meet your rate.

Adjust Your Rate as You Grow: Regularly review and adjust your hourly rate as your skills and market value increase. Focus on tasks that challenge you and align with your new rate.

Value Your Time: Treat your time as your most valuable asset. Systematically eliminate tasks that don't maximize the value of your time. Focus on activities that produce significant results and align with your long-term goals.

By following these steps, you can effectively conserve your energy and ensure that your time is spent on the most impactful activities. This will lead to increased income, improved skills, and greater marketability.

Leveraged Action Steps

Conserve your power by completing the exercise modeled in the Reality Check section here.

	Daily Tasks	Hourly Rate (for that task)	Action (Prioritize, Outsource, Eliminate, Deprioritize)
#1			
#2			
#3			
#4			
#5			
#6			

Chapter Ten Takeaway

LAW TEN

Conserve your power. Outsource,
eliminate, or deprioritize all tasks
that don't drive the most results.

Swim With the Tide

"You can't stop the waves, but
you can learn how to surf."

—Jon Kabat-Zinn (American professor of medicine and mindfulness)

When I was eight or nine years old, my brother and I were sucked into an ocean rip current. The vast expanse of the ocean stretched out before us and was welcoming at first, but then, without warning, the calm blue sea developed an undertow more powerful than our little arms and legs could handle. Those frantic moments felt like an eternity. We exhausted every last ounce of energy fighting the rip current and felt like we would surely drown. It must have taken us thirty minutes to break free of the tide, but we finally made it to shore, drained of energy and reluctant to do any other activities for the rest of the day.

Decades later, with the wisdom that only age and experience bring, I looked back on that day and recognized the lesson we missed in the moment. Instead of fighting the powerful waters, if we had simply gone with the flow and let the current carry us deeper into its waters for a moment, we could have used the same current to return to shore. The power of the rip current that once threatened us would have been our ticket back to safety. It's a humbling realization: We were fighting a force that, if properly understood, could have been our ally.

Isn't that often the case in life?

Similarly, judo practitioners harness their opponent's energy and balance and use it to their advantage rather than absorbing their blows directly. They redirect that energy and turn their challenges into opportunities. In the same way, we should strive to embrace and use every challenge we encounter to our advantage.

When we face challenges, our instinct is to resist and fight back with all our might. But sometimes the secret is to harness the power of the situation, go with the flow, and redirect that energy to our advantage. Life's riptides—its unexpected setbacks and trials—can either drain us or drive us forward, depending on how we navigate them. The key is to recognize and use it as leverage rather than fight against it.

Harness the Trend, Make a Killing

Many success stories point to the entrepreneur's ability to correctly identify an emerging trend, understand changing consumer behavior, or articulate latent needs and unmet demands.

One such story is that of Reed Hastings. Netflix was born because its founder recognized the growing demand for DVD rentals. Netflix has continued to thrive because Reed has consistently capitalized on consumer trends.[38]

But let's rewind that old VHS tape back to 1997.

The go-to provider for movie rentals in 1997 was Blockbuster, and it was pretty amazing; they had tons of titles and tons of customers.

However, those who returned movies late were fined, which meant that a significant portion of their customer base was paying late fees. In fact, Blockbuster made about $800 million (16 percent of its total revenue) in late fees in 2000.

One customer who paid his fair share of late fees was Reed. One day, a $40 fine made him angry enough to create a better way.

Reed teamed up with his friend Marc Randolph to find a solution. They realized that DVDs, which were hot in Japan at the time, would soon replace the VHS tapes prevalent at Blockbuster, so they started a company similar to Blockbuster but focused on renting DVDs. The main difference was that they would not charge late fees. You paid a flat monthly fee and got your DVD rentals delivered to your door, just like any other subscription. Netflix was incorporated in the fall of 1997 with $1.9 million in seed funding and Reed and Marc at the helm.

In the early days, Netflix offered unlimited access to content for $19.95, with about 900 titles in stock. DVDs came in red envelopes, and Netflix paid for the postage. Subscribers could create a "queue" and choose the order in which DVDs would be sent to them. They would receive the next DVD as soon as the previous one was returned. Within five years, Netflix was stocking thousands of titles and shipping millions of DVDs every day. In 2000, Reed even went to John Antioco, the former CEO of Blockbuster, and offered to sell Netflix for $50 million, but he was turned down.

This turned out to be a big mistake for Blockbuster.

Netflix hit a million subscribers that same year and went public the following year, raising $82.1 million at an IPO valuation of $309.7 million.

The next chapter of growth made Netflix the company we know today. **Reed Hastings saw and embraced the shift from traditional DVD rentals to online streaming.** It began streaming content directly to televisions, computers, and tablets. This premiered through a service called Watch Now. It was so successful that Netflix shifted its focus to streaming, prompting Reed to release an official statement: "Three years ago, we were a DVD-by-mail company that offered some streaming. Now we are a streaming company that also offers DVD by mail."

They had ridden the waves, not fought them.

Netflix made its next move in the streaming business in 2012 with the launch of original shows like *House of Cards*. Since then, they have produced over 1,900 original titles, including *Squid Game* and *The Crown*, which have become global sensations. Netflix is now available in over 190 countries, offering content in thousands of languages to over 209 million subscribers. Netflix now competes with the likes of HBO Max and Disney Plus and has an annual revenue of over $25 billion.

It was only last year or so that the company began to take on serious losses because of customer habits (such as password sharing) and began exploring new revenue streams (such as paying for ad-free viewing). The latest wave decreased its profitability. Netflix is currently trying to get onto the right side of the waves of change one more time. As movie theaters become less popular, Netflix is taking action to regain its competitive edge. The streaming landscape is flooded with original content, and Netflix must differentiate itself by consistently delivering fresh, engaging content. This isn't just a concern for Netflix—it's a challenge we all must address. We must adapt and evolve to stay relevant and retain our audience.

Sink or Swim

The same year that Netflix shifted gears and became a full-fledged streaming company, Blockbuster filed for bankruptcy.

Blockbuster was there before Netflix, HBO Go, and Amazon Prime Video. In its prime, Blockbuster employed 84,000 people, generated $6 billion in revenue, and had thousands of customers visiting 9,000 store locations. Blockbuster failed to adapt to the digital streaming trend, which meant that DVDs and VHS tapes would no longer be required for movie access. Instead of adapting to the market trends, it just kept charging customers for late fees to remain profitable. A former executive at Blockbuster even stated, "Digital would have changed Blockbuster's business, for sure, but it wasn't its killer. That credit belongs to Blockbuster itself."[32]

The first mistake was not buying Netflix for $50 million. Just a few years later, Blockbuster was struggling with sales revenue and legal issues. They lost $518 million in 2009 and were delisted from the New York Stock Exchange a few months later. Over the next three years, its DVD mail services ended, partnerships folded, and video stores shut down—now just one remains. The standalone store still has roughly 4,000 loyal customers and many more tourists who drop by out of nostalgia.

While Netflix was making the shift from physical to digital content because they understood that millennials didn't care about DVDs or CDs anymore, Blockbuster's only strategic move was to open more video stores. Stores that would soon become obsolete. Blockbuster did eventually add services (such as rental kiosks) to make things easier for consumers, but these offerings failed to keep pace with the trends of the time.

The concept of *adapt or die* has been a reality since the dawn of humanity. As John F. Kennedy wisely said, "Change is the law of life. And those who look only to the past or present are certain to miss the future." It's often not the strongest or smartest people who succeed the most when change occurs, but those who are most adaptable to it.

Those who refuse to change can die, no matter how big they are.

Those who do change, and change faster than the others, can leverage time—and build substantial wealth.

When Tsunamis Come, Build Ships

When 2020 dawned with the shadow of the COVID pandemic, the U.S. government's money presses ran wild, ushering in a tidal wave of inflation. Some of my astute associates promptly exchanged all their paper cash for tangible assets like lumber, oil, and steel. Their foresight wasn't just about the obvious supply and demand dynamic. They knew the rising tide of currency would dilute their dollar's worth. They made a smart move by acquiring tangible assets to protect themselves against the devaluation of the dollar. And three years later, their assumptions paid off, keeping them from losing their hard-earned equity.

I did the same. I bought the most expensive investment property the bank would lend on to ride the wave of inflation that was about to dilute my hard-earned cash. Debt is one of the best ways to protect yourself from inflation because you only have to pay back the number of dollars you borrowed, not the actual value behind the dollars you borrowed. If you spent $100K buying 100K widgets and inflation diluted your currency by 50 percent, you could sell the 100K widgets for $200K, pay back the $100K, and keep the 50 percent difference. Even though the currency changed, the value of the widgets remained constant.

We must look to the future and embrace the technological shifts and changes to consumer purchasing preferences. It's crucial to recognize when an industry has fundamentally shifted and have the courage to pivot toward the future.

The Internet marked the beginning of the end for many traditional paper-based industries. Those who clung to outdated business models were left behind. Visionaries who embraced digital transformation thrived. The lesson here is clear: Don't hold on to dying trends. Once you know your industry is doomed, follow the future.

The rapid decline of brick-and-mortar retail stores in the face of e-commerce giants like Amazon is a clear example of this. Those who swiftly transitioned to online platforms, investing in digital infrastructure and logistics, captured new market shares and sustained their businesses. Those who resisted the shift saw their revenues plummet as consumer behavior changed irrevocably. Anticipating and adapting to technological shifts is essential for maintaining relevance and ensuring long-term success.

The rise of renewable energy is a modern-day tsunami. The world is moving away from fossil fuels and toward sustainable energy sources, and savvy investors are seizing the opportunity to invest in this sector. Investing in solar, wind, and other renewable energy technologies is the smart move. It aligns with global environmental goals and positions investors to benefit from the inevitable transition away from traditional energy sources.

Look at the foresight of the early adopters in the renewable energy sector. Those who invested in solar farms, wind turbines, and green technology companies have seen substantial returns on their investments. They built ships to navigate the green energy tsunami, and they are now reaping the benefits of a world increasingly focused on sustainability.

The financial technology (fintech) revolution is here, and it's going to change the way industries operate. Traditional banking and financial services are being disrupted by innovative fintech solutions that offer greater efficiency, accessibility, and user experience—and this is happening at a rapid pace. Investors who recognized this shift and allocated resources to fintech startups are now part of a rapidly growing industry that will redefine financial transactions globally.

Those who clung to conventional banking models are witnessing a decline in their market share as consumers and businesses gravitate toward fintech solutions. Embrace the change, and invest in the future. This is the key to maintaining and growing wealth when faced with transformative technological advancements.

In every era, there are moments when the world changes so dramatically that only those who adapt can survive and thrive. Build ships when tsunamis come. That's the lesson of every era, from the global pandemic to the rise of the Internet, the shift to renewable energy, or the fintech revolution. Understand and leverage these waves of change to position yourself for exponential growth in an ever-evolving landscape.

Change is inevitable, but each wave of disruption carries new opportunities. Even if you miss one, another will follow. While it's easy to resent or resist these waves, why not embrace them? By moving the ebb and flow of the tide, we ensure that we'll always win with ease.

Aligning Skill Sets with Opportunities

Two of my favorite entrepreneurs, Alex Hormozi and Russell Brunson, have a framework for creating exponential wealth by aligning skill sets with the right opportunities. They believe that success comes from acquiring skills and then properly aligning those skills with the right opportunities. This alignment is essential for maximizing potential.

Think of measuring a person's skills on a scale of 1 to 10. Skill Levels 1 through 3 include basic skills that require minimal training, such as basic customer service or entry-level administrative tasks. These basic skills are essential starting points but have limited earning potential. As individuals progress to Levels 4 through 6, they develop intermediate skills that require more experience and understanding. These include proficient use of specialized software and managing small teams. These skills are more complex and open doors to more substantial opportunities.

At Levels 7 through 9, individuals have advanced skills. These are rare and valuable skills characterized by a high degree of specialization and sophistication, honed over years of experience. Expert-level programming and managing large projects are just two examples.

And Level 10 is the ultimate achievement of mastery as a leader or innovator in your field. It's the level of excellence achieved by world-class surgeons or top-tier CEOs.

The same is true for industries and opportunities. There are Level 1 opportunities with limited income potential, and there are Level 10 industries and opportunities with lots of potential. Typically, the higher-level opportunities are in new, cutting-edge fields, or they have superior scale and leverage.

This matters because if you have Level 7 skills but are working a Level 3 job, your income is capped. It's not your fault; it's because your industry or position isn't designed to compensate for your higher skill level. Let's be real. Many people with Level 3 skills get Level 3 jobs and over time become Level 7 operators, but they're stuck at a Level 3 income because they're still in a Level 3 job.

I've met Level 8 operators working Level 2 opportunities who make less than the Level 3 skill set people who got lucky and are working a Level 8 or 9 job.

Your industry and job opportunities matter.

The key to leveraging these concepts is to match your current skill level with the appropriate opportunity level. Mismatches create significant challenges. It may be difficult to land a high-level opportunity if you are building on low-level skills. If you're overqualified for a low-level opportunity, you're not maximizing your potential. To achieve optimal success, you must seek opportunities that match your current skill level.

As your skills develop from basic to mastery, you must progressively seek higher level opportunities. Start with Level 1 through 3 opportunities to develop basic skills. As you acquire intermediate skills, find Level 4 through 6 opportunities to enable further growth. Advanced skills must be matched with high-impact opportunities at Levels 7 through 9. And when you achieve mastery, I hope you go out and change the world!

Aligning your skills with the right opportunities allows you to strategically navigate your career, ensuring continuous development and full utilization of your abilities. This approach leads to greater job satisfaction, career growth, and overall success—all of which are foundational to exponential wealth.

Reality Check:

Are you riding the right wave?

Ride the waves of opportunity. Just as a skilled sailor harnesses the wind and current to navigate the sea, so too must we align our efforts with the prevailing trends and opportunities of our chosen fields.

Swimming with the tide means aligning your efforts with the natural flow of opportunity. Don't fight the current. Move with it. Let the forces that propel you forward carry you to success. Identify and capitalize on the trends, technologies, and market dynamics that are gaining momentum. Start with a thorough analysis of your industry. Identify the technological advances, consumer preferences, and regulatory changes driving growth. By understanding these trends, you will be in position to capitalize on the opportunities they present.

One of the easiest ways to control your environment is to simply change environments. Pick the industries that offer the best opportunities.

As an entrepreneur, swimming with the tide may mean that it's time to pivot to remain competitive. It may be painful, but be open to changing your business model, product offerings, or target market to better align with emerging opportunities. You must regularly evaluate your business and its position in the marketplace. You need to identify new technologies or customer needs that you can address more effectively. Take bold steps to reposition your business for greater success: Launch that new product, target that new buyer, or scrap that marketing tactic that just isn't working anymore.

As an employee, swimming with the tide may look like searching for opportunities in new markets or industries. Transitioning to a growing field can open doors to more fulfilling work and higher earnings. If your current industry is declining, start talking to people in new industries to find ones that are booming and need your skills and talents. Network, go to expensive business conferences, and meet people who are ahead of you. Seek out and apply for jobs that offer more potential: Take that online course, attend that workshop, and master that skill set.

Be open to change and be willing to pivot when necessary. Evaluate your career path regularly and make strategic moves to position yourself in high-potential industries. Seek out opportunities—don't wait for them to come to you. Adapt to your environment and seize every opportunity to turn it to your advantage.

Don't fight the tide. Ride it.

Leveraged Action Steps

The biggest trends are the biggest opportunities. Find them.

	Leveraged Action Steps	Growth Opportunity
#1	Does anyone at your company make more than you? If so, why? How can you position yourself to earn what they do? Identify any skill gaps you would need to close to achieve this.	

#2	Do any of your friends make more than you?	
	If so, why?	
	How can you position yourself to earn what they do?	
	Identify any skill gaps you would need to close to achieve this.	
#3	Search LinkedIn (and other social media channels).	
	Are any of your acquaintances (in similar fields) making more than you?	
	If so, why?	
	How can you position yourself to earn what they do?	
	Identify any skill gaps you would need to close to achieve this.	

Chapter Eleven Takeaway

LAW ELEVEN
DON'T FIGHT THE TIDE OF
CONSUMER TRENDS. RIDE IT.

Ride the Coattails of Success

"It's good to work for other people. I worked for others for twenty years. They paid me to learn."

—Vera Wang (celebrity fashion designer)

Are you familiar with Steve Ballmer? If not, let me paint a picture for you. Steve Ballmer, the former Microsoft executive, is one of the most enthusiastic and passionate figures in the tech world—and arguably in all of business. You may recognize him from his unforgettable, high-energy performances on stage. At Microsoft's twenty-fifth anniversary celebration, he famously shouted, "I love this company!" with the kind of excitement most people reserve for winning the lottery. Or maybe you've seen the viral clip of him feverishly chanting, "Developers, developers, developers!" over and over, sweating profusely, and relentlessly pacing back and forth across the stage.[40] His larger-than-life presence has left a lasting mark on tech culture.

Here's what you need to know if you've never heard of him: He's worth $148 billion, according to the Bloomberg Billionaires Index 2024, and is the eighth-richest man in the world—without ever having founded a company.[41]

Ballmer was born in Michigan. His father was a manager at Ford, and his mother was the daughter of an immigrant merchant. He went to Harvard (where he lived down the hall from Bill Gates). Shortly after graduating, he joined Procter & Gamble as an assistant product manager, spent a few years trying to write screenplays for Hollywood, and then went to Stanford for an MBA. He left to join Microsoft as its thirtieth employee and the first manager hired by Gates, with a salary of $50K and an 8 percent stake in the company. From 1980 to the 2000s, he led and built Microsoft's various verticals (sales, support, operations, development, etc.) and effectively grew to become Bill Gates's number two before being named CEO for the next fourteen years. Today, Ballmer owns the Los Angeles Clippers of the NBA.

While Ballmer has a strong entrepreneurial streak, he never went the founder route. Instead, he joined an early startup and rode the coattails of success straight to the top.

The Contributor Mindset

I opened this chapter with a quote from the renowned fashion designer, Vera Wang. The daughter of immigrant Chinese parents, Wang's career path in NYC took her from figure skating to editing at Vogue to working for Ralph Lauren before deciding to launch her own bridal fashion design company at the age of forty.[42] For two decades, her aim wasn't to build her own brand but to *learn from the best.*

Many of the most successful entrepreneurs in the world never set out to be founders—at least not at the beginning. Their primary goal was to learn, contribute, and serve. Many of those who went on to become successful founders did so by leveraging the knowledge, relationships, and networks they formed while working for others and then built on the success of their former employers.

Falguni Nayar's story is another prime example of the contributor's mindset leading to amazing things. Nayar is India's richest self-made woman, as of 2022.[43] She has had a diverse career, including roles in management consulting, investment banking, and serving as managing director at Kotak Mahindra Capital. At the age of fifty, she founded Nykaa, an online beauty retail platform, and succeeded by leveraging her extensive network and experience. Nykaa now serves over 40 percent of India's beauty market. Her vast connections and relationships are what made this possible.

There are countless examples of businesspeople climbing the corporate ladder for decades, learning and aligning with the best in their fields before choosing to venture out on their own.

The Challenge of Being a Founder

Sometimes, it feels like *everyone* on social media is launching their own businesses. Data from Global Entrepreneurship Monitor backs this up; there's been a rise in entrepreneurship since the 2000s.[44] This could be attributed to progress in technology, more political support for businesses, the rise of the gig economy, or simply because we have celebrity entrepreneurs like Gary Vaynerchuk documenting their daily lives as entrepreneurs for the whole world to see. When HGTV rose in popularity, everyone wanted to flip houses. Now that thousands of entrepreneurs have YouTube channels, lots of people have joined that bandwagon. Overall, I think the shift from mindless entertainment to entrepreneurial entertainment has been massively positive and has inspired people to do great things that make the world a better place.

Roughly 49 to 67 percent of millennials and 41 to 76 percent of Gen Zers say they would like to be entrepreneurs.[45] That's about half of all millennials and Gen Zers combined.

One of the challenges with this is that the data shows the average successful startup founder is forty-five years old (with people like Mark Zuckerberg, Steve Jobs, and Bill Gates being the exception, not the norm).[46] Meanwhile, the average age of millennials and Gen Zers who want to be entrepreneurs is 26.5. This gap is precisely why riding the coattails of success can be so helpful.

I love entrepreneurship. I firmly believe it's one of the most powerful forces for positive change in our world. However, it's a challenging path to pursue, especially now that everyone wants a piece of the action. People often underestimate the pain tolerance required to build a successful company. They also assume that launching their own company is the only path to serious wealth, but this is simply not true. Many people working regular jobs buy the victory (Law Six) and buy assets (which we'll talk about in Law Thirteen) and become wealthy that way.

Many individuals have become massively successful by aligning themselves with the right people at the right time and contributing to their endeavors, instead of striking out on their own. Expanding an established company is easier than creating one from scratch. These individuals often have a clear understanding of their strengths and weaknesses, respect for those they align with, and a realistic grasp of the resources and qualities needed to build a company from scratch. So, they join forces with entrepreneurs who are already taking the leap.

By doing so, they benefit from a lot of the upside of entrepreneurship, without a lot of the uncertainty.

If you want to launch your own company, do it. Do it for the right reasons, and do it at the *right time*. Don't do it just because you think it's the only path to wealth. It's not.

For the rest of us, riding the coattails of others' successes has many advantages. You get paid to develop the skills you need to succeed while building a network of peers, mentors, and future investors. You have the financial freedom to develop specialized knowledge in a field, so you know where the gaps in the marketplace are. You will learn from others' mistakes (on their dime), and save valuable time not making them yourself. This is especially true if you're in the early stages of your career. And lastly, you build a solid financial foundation so you can afford to ride the waves of risk that will come along when you build your company.

Becoming Invaluable

If you do decide to ride the coattails of success (and I hope you do, at least for a little while), do not expect it to be a cakewalk. One challenge you must overcome to align yourself with successful people is that the elite are often overwhelmed with staffing options for their teams. Be under no delusion: *The elite don't need you.* You must give them a compelling reason to let you ride their coattails.

Let me tell you about my buddy, Pedro. He has mastered the art of carving out opportunities where seemingly none exist. Pedro's journey to success is legendary. His story didn't start with a grand job offer; in fact, it was quite the opposite. He was rejected from the job he really wanted. But rather than accepting his fate, Pedro took a proactive approach. He boldly asked the CEO who turned him down one of my favorite questions: "Tell me, what is the biggest challenge in your business right now?"

The CEO revealed that the company was flooded with leads who weren't actively engaging with their offerings. Pedro saw this as an opportunity and got to work, immersing himself in research and case studies from companies that had overcome similar hurdles. To make a long story short, Pedro solved the problem and proved himself to be an invaluable asset to the company. Shortly thereafter, he was offered a role—a role that, mind you, was created out of thin air, specifically for him.

As the firm expanded, Pedro consistently identified and proactively solved the newest bottlenecks the company faced. He elevated himself to a position where he has access to countless celebrities and influential businesspeople. By making himself invaluable to one influential person and leveraging his successes, he gained access to hundreds of influential people and a world of opportunities.

Identifying as an Entrepreneur

Even though I've never started a company and may never start a company, I'm still an entrepreneur. This statement has often confused people, but I can assure you that I am 100 percent an entrepreneur.

I don't need "founder" in my email signature to embody the entrepreneurial spirit and work like I own the business.

I have no interest in launching my own company. There's no question that being employee number ten at a startup carries far less risk than having your name on the door. Ninety percent of startups fail. I wanted to find a career path that allowed me to strategically avoid unnecessary risk while still earning a piece of the pie. So I've decided that I would much rather help a young startup grow—in ways only I can—than to found a startup myself. By working to boost startups that have already weathered their initial storms, I get to flex my entrepreneurial muscles, make big things happen, and take my portion of profits without exposing myself to potential failure.

My strategy has paid off.

I have never been part of a failed startup. And even if that were to happen, I am confident in my ability to pivot and find another promising venture. That's the beauty of riding the coattails of success. If they win, you win. If they lose, you sidestep their losses, pivot, and find a new win. It's that simple.

Some might say I'm missing out on a huge financial windfall by not founding the company myself. That may be true, but I'm not taking that risk. I'm trading that uncertainty for a more predictable path that matches my risk appetite. I'm leveraging someone else's success to give me the capital I need to buy the assets I use to support my family. So instead of building the primary business from the ground up, I'm riding the coattails of success, which I then use to buy hard assets like commercial real estate, oil wells, intellectual property, and other assets that pay me monthly. This strategy has worked well for me and allows me to be an owner without being the founder.

I've found a way to ride the coattails of success.

How will you do the same?

Reality Check

No one's going to invite you.

Here's the straightforward takeaway for this law: If you admire someone's business and want to work with them, don't wait for an invitation.

You're not getting one!

Take the initiative. Do the homework. Give them solutions and solve their problems.

And here's the scary part: Do it without expecting anything in return.

So many people make the mistake of helping someone with strings attached. Solve their problems without asking for anything in return, and keep doing it until they feel embarrassed at how much free work they've gotten from you. I know it might be scary to give someone free labor without a guaranteed return, but the upside (when this works) will completely overshadow anything you gave away in the process.

Leveraged Action Steps

Explore ways you can ride the coattails of success. Find paths that align with your strengths and make them your own.

	Leveraged Action Steps	Your Notes
#1	**Identify Your Future Successes:** List three entrepreneurs who will most likely be massive successes one day. (LinkedIn is a great place to find them.)	
#2	**Assess Your Strengths:** What skills do you bring to the table that these entrepreneurs need?	
#3	**Solve Problems Proactively:** Solve a problem for one of these entrepreneurs without them asking you to.	
#4	**Align Your Contributions:** Show them how you can contribute to their desired result.	

Chapter Twelve Takeaway

LAW TWELVE

ALIGN YOURSELF WITH SUCCESSFUL
PEOPLE TO LEVERAGE THEIR SUCCESS.

Buy Assets; Limit Liabilities

"Assets create wealth; liabilities destroy it."

—Unknown

Picture this: You're sitting in a small, cluttered office, surrounded by piles of bills, living paycheck to paycheck, and feeling the weight of the world on your shoulders. It may not be that hard to imagine—you might be living it right now. This is the sad reality for a staggering 62 percent of Americans as of 2023. More than half of Americans are struggling under the weight of liabilities like mortgages, car loans, and credit card debt.[47] It's a relentless treadmill—endless work with no financial progress.

But despite that, there is a smaller subset of our population that has come to the simple yet profound realization that the key to financial freedom isn't about earning more. Real financial freedom comes from owning assets that put money *in* your pocket each month while limiting the liabilities that take money *out* of your pocket every month.

Now, imagine a different scene. It's early morning, and you're sipping coffee on the porch of your beautiful duplex. The rent from one half of the duplex covers your mortgage, relieving you of that burden. Your car is fully paid off. Each month, you receive multiple checks for work you didn't actively participate in. You've stepped off the relentless treadmill and no longer feel like you're endlessly pushing a boulder uphill. Instead, you're on a path lined with golden assets leading you to financial liberation.

In this chapter, we'll explore how to make this shift—how to *buy assets* and *limit liabilities*. I'll help you distinguish between true assets and the hidden liabilities that masquerade as assets. I'll also show you how to turn your biggest monthly expenses, like home mortgages, boats, or vacation homes, into more than just financial burdens.

Before we get into the nitty-gritty, I want you to ask yourself an important question: Are you ready to shift your focus from short-term pleasures to long-term treasures? Since you're reading this book, I'm going to presume that the answer is a resounding yes. Let this chapter be your guide to help you transform your financial *drains* into financial *gains*.

Defining Key Terms

To navigate the financial racetrack effectively, you need to understand the subtle distinctions between assets, liabilities, and investments. Let's break these down with real-life examples for a clearer understanding.

Assets

Definition: An asset is something that puts money in your pocket. It could be a stock that pays dividends, a rental property generating income, or an automated side business that puts cash in your pocket each month.

Example: Sarah is a schoolteacher. She might not make a lot of money, but she's smart with what she has. Sarah bought a condo and rents it. The rental income covers the mortgage, pays for the management company, and provides her with a little extra cash each month. Sarah's condo is a classic example of an asset—it pays her every month without her active involvement.

Liabilities

Definition: A liability takes money out of your pocket. This includes things like personal car loans, credit card debt, and mortgages on your primary residence.

Example: Tom loves sports cars. He bought a high-end sports car on loan. The car is fun, but the payments, insurance, and maintenance costs take money out of his pocket. Tom also finds himself doing a lot of the repairs himself to *save* money. This consumes a considerable amount of time and distracts him from improving his family's situation. Tom's sports car is a classic example of a liability—it costs him time and takes money out of his pocket every month.

Investments

Definition: An investment is something you buy with the hope that it will increase in value over time. People often mistake investments for assets, but the key difference is that investments don't generate immediate cash flow.

Example: Lucy invested in a collection of fine art and cryptocurrency. While the art and bitcoin may appreciate over time, they do not generate income for her now. Therefore, they're investments, not assets.

The Wealth Foot Race: Assets Versus Liabilities

Let's start with a story that might sound familiar. Meet Emily, a young professional with a love for the latest gadgets and fashion. She viewed her salary as a means to acquire the finer things in life—a new car, the latest smartphone, and designer outfits. However, despite her impressive income, Emily felt stuck, barely making a dent in her student loans and other obligations.

Now, consider Jack, a colleague of Emily's with a similar income. Instead of splurging, Jack focused on investing his surplus cash into things that would pay him. He bought a modest car and lived in a modest apartment, channeling his savings into rental properties, oil and gas syndications, and ATM funds. While Emily rushed to achieve short-term victories, Jack deliberately built up assets that would support his future lifestyle.

Five years down the line, Emily's race became more challenging. The thrill of new purchases had faded, leaving her no closer to financial freedom. Meanwhile, Jack's assets were growing with time. His rental properties had appreciated, and his share of the ATM and oil funds were generating steady streams of income.

Think of your financial journey as a foot race. Liabilities are ankle weights slowing you down. Assets are the wind at your back, pushing you forward. It's about pacing, not sprinting; building, not spending.

Now, don't get me wrong—I'm not here to convince you not to buy the nice things you want. Quite the opposite. The goal is to buy the assets first, so those assets can fund the luxuries later. When you prioritize building wealth, you'll be able to afford the things you love without sacrificing your future.

Transforming Liabilities into Assets

Magical things happen when you turn liabilities into assets. Here are some real-life examples of how to achieve this transformation.

Case Study 1: The Homeowners' Shift

Background: Amanda and Jake, a young couple, bought a home with a sizable mortgage. While their home was a dream come true, the mortgage was a monthly drain on their finances.

Transformation: They converted their basement into a rental apartment. The rent they now collect covers more than half of their mortgage payment.

Step-by-Step Guide:

1. Evaluate your home for potential rental spaces, including basements, spare rooms, or garages that can be converted into rentable apartments.
2. Obtain the necessary permits to make the space rentable, or rent it out to a friend or family member to avoid the permit process entirely.
3. Market the rental space effectively, and screen tenants carefully to ensure a steady and reliable rental income.

Challenges and Solutions:

- **Potential Challenge:** You may face high upfront renovation costs, depending on your situation.

- **Solution:** Get a home improvement loan at a low interest rate. Renovate your space and pay it off quickly with your new rental income.

Case Study 2: From Leisure to Lucrative

Background: Raj owned a luxury boat that he used only a few times a year; it was incurring significant maintenance and docking fees.

Transformation: Raj turned his seldom-used luxury boat into a profitable asset by renting it out for private events and tours.

Step-by-Step Guide:

1. Research the market demand for boat rentals in your area.
2. Ensure your boat meets all safety and regulatory standards.
3. List your boat on rental platforms with clear, attractive descriptions and photos.
4. Provide excellent service and proactively ask for reviews so you can rent your boat consistently.
5. If, for whatever reason, you can't rent your boat out for a profit, sell your boat for a loss to stop the bleeding.

Challenges and Solutions:

- **Potential Challenge:** Balancing personal use with rental availability.

- **Solution:** Create a schedule to balance your personal enjoyment of the boat with peak rental times.

Case Study 3: Vacation Home Turnaround

Background: Emily had a vacation home she used only a few weeks each year that had ongoing costs.

Transformation: She turned it into a short-term rental property managed by a property management company.

Step-by-Step Guide:

1. Evaluate the potential of your vacation home as a short-term or long-term rental.
2. Make any necessary updates or improvements to appeal to guests.
3. Choose a reliable property management company to handle bookings and maintenance.
4. Market the property on popular vacation rental sites.

Challenges and Solutions:

- **Potential Challenge:** Property damage and maintenance concerns.

- **Solution:** Insure your property to cover damages, and make sure it will have enough cash flow to cover the mortgage if/when your space needs repairs.

- **Pro Tip:** Hire someone else to manage your property. People often fall into the *self-management* trap to save money and increase profits. Remember, it's only leveraged income if you don't spend time on it. Otherwise, you just bought yourself another job.

Case Study 4: Investment to Asset Transformation

Background: James owns $200K in stocks and cryptocurrency. While these investments have appreciated significantly, they do not provide a steady monthly income. As a result, James still relies on his employer to pay his bills and is no closer to achieving financial freedom.

Transformation: James sold his stocks and cryptocurrency to purchase income-generating assets that provide him with regular monthly payments. These monthly checks cover his immediate bills and allow James to pursue other endeavors.

Step-by-Step Guide:

1. Sell your investments.
2. Buy assets. (It's that simple!)

Challenges and Solutions:

- **Potential Challenge:** Capital gains tax could cost you a significant portion of your profit.

- **Solution:** Use Law Seventeen (Don't Own Anything on Paper) and leverage bonus depreciation to write off your capital gains. This allows you to keep most, if not all, of your profit when you sell.

These case studies show how you can creatively turn your liabilities into profitable assets. Take these examples and apply them to your own situation.

Tackle your liabilities aggressively; don't let them drain your resources. I'm not suggesting that you cut everything, but you'll find that life is much easier when your money is flowing in rather than out. Even if you just cancel a few unnecessary subscriptions and turn one liability into an asset, you will feel the difference. Do you feel that relief when you have some financial breathing room? That's called financial peace, and it's amazing.

Reality Check

Your financial racetrack.

Take a moment to fill out the table below.

On the left side, list your liabilities—things like home mortgages, car payments, debts, and anything else that takes money out of your pocket each month.

In the middle, list your investments—things like saving accounts, stocks, gold, bitcoin, and anything you own that's appreciating in value (but doesn't create cash flow).

On the right side, list your assets—things like rental properties, syndicated real estate funds, equity shares, royalties, and anything else that puts money in your pocket.

This is your financial racetrack. Which side is heavier? Are you weighed down by liabilities or propelled by assets?

Warren Buffett once said, "If you buy things you do not need, soon you will have to sell things you need." This simple wisdom highlights the importance of discerning between wants and needs, between short-lived pleasures and long-term dreams. It's not about what you make. It's about how hard your money works for you and how many generations after you get to benefit from it.

Your mission (should you choose to accept it) is to offload as many liabilities from your piece of paper as possible within the next six months. You might also want to convert some of your investments into assets to increase your monthly cash flow.

As you complete this exercise, ask yourself: Are you ready to make your life easier by transforming your liabilities and investments into assets?

The race to financial freedom is long if you're dragging liabilities with you. Make your race easier by completing the following exercise.

Leveraged Action Steps

Write down your liabilities, investments, and assets. Systematically convert your liabilities and investments into assets over the next six months. (If you need practical steps for acquiring assets, see Law Seventeen.)

Liabilities	Investments	Assets
#1		
#2		
#3		
#4		
#5		
#6		

Chapter Thirteen Takeaway

LAW THIRTEEN
MAKE LIFE EASY. LIMIT YOUR LIABILITIES.
USE YOUR INVESTMENTS TO BUY ASSETS.

Create Once; Sell Forever

"Learn to sell. Learn to build. If you can do both, you will be unstoppable."

—Naval Ravikant (angel investor and author)

Benzodiazepines, or "benzos," have been around since the 1950s, offering relief for anxiety and insomnia. However, it wasn't until the 1980s that Xanax, the most potent and fast-acting benzo on the market, emerged. Its appeal was not limited to those with severe conditions. Even individuals with mild anxiety found solace in its calming effects. Xanax quickly rose to prominence and became one of the top-selling psychiatric drugs by the 1990s. Today, this single drug generates about $200 million annually for Pfizer.[48]

To put this in perspective: a tablet developed decades ago by a single chemist is now prescribed fifty million times a year worldwide.

This demand will not likely diminish anytime soon. Xanax's enduring success illustrates a crucial law of leverage: Create something remarkable once and sell it perpetually.

An Age of Infinity

The Industrial Revolution was the catalyst for incredible growth in manufacturing and empowered companies like Pfizer to produce and sell products at a scale that was not previously possible. This era revolutionized manufacturing and marked a pivotal shift from handcrafted items to mass production of machine-made goods.

A human laborer can only produce so much in an hour. Machines can do a whole lot more. And so, with industrialization, we saw the emergence of something called *economies of scale*. Production operations got larger, safer, faster, and more efficient—especially in monetary terms. As companies manufactured and sold more goods, they were able to spread out their investment costs (such as machines and equipment) to create high-quality goods cheaply.

Pharmaceutical companies make a fortune because for every one-time investment in research and development to create a product like Xanax, they can manufacture and sell millions of pills at a tiny fraction of the cost. This cycle can continue for a very long time until it is replaced by the next bestseller.

Starbucks created a product people like, and they are currently opening more than six hundred new identical locations a year.[49]

Boeing and Airbus do the same thing with their aircraft. For instance, Boeing developed the 737 airplane in the 1960s and has sold over 11,000 of these aircraft to airlines around the world.

Apple has sold over 1.5 billion iPhones since Steve Jobs created the first one in 2007.[50]

Now, obviously, these last two companies made some modifications along the way—updating designs, adding new features, and improving technology—but each new development allowed them to sell even more units. With every tweak or innovation, they attract new customers while continuing to sell to their loyal base, fueling growth with each iteration.

We live in a time with almost infinite scale. This is the first time in human history that it's been possible to make something once and sell it millions of times.

Physical to Digital

As we see from big pharma, industrialization was a *big* deal for manufacturing physical goods. Unlike humans, machines could keep working with minimal human supervision. There were, however, limitations with mass manufacturing. Although advanced machinery significantly increased our output for products, it still had limits to what it could produce because of space and raw materials.

The digital business, however, is not constrained by these limitations.

The 1990s Internet revolution made scale possible in ways we never could have imagined. Even the best salesman in the world can only work, say, a maximum of sixty to eighty hours a week consistently. Now, compare this to its digital counterpart—an e-commerce store's landing page. It can stay open and run ads all day, all night, twenty-four hours a day, seven days a week, all year long, at a fraction of the cost. More importantly, it has a much wider reach, and there are no geographical or language restrictions when it comes to attracting potential customers.

If the Industrial Revolution made products scalable, the Digital Revolution made them hyper-scalable.

Take the case of Salesforce. Salesforce builds and sells software and apps that help businesses stay on top of their customer relationships, using data and technology. Salesforce generated $31 billion in revenue this past fiscal year. The largest single chunk of this revenue, $8 billion, came from one product called Sales Cloud, which was engineered and launched all the way back in 2009.[51]

MasterClass is a prime example of this principle. As a digital learning platform featuring celebrity instructors, MasterClass collaborates with experts, records their teachings, and sells these video courses to millions of subscribers for $180 each.

People are all too eager to pay for filmmaking lessons from Martin Scorsese, photography tips from Annie Leibovitz, or creativity advice from Anna Wintour. Chris Voss's negotiation course has had over 22 million views. MasterClass, which started with $1.9 million in seed funding, made nearly $94 million in sales for 2022.[52]

What we see here is that companies like Pfizer, Salesforce, and MasterClass invest millions to develop the first product. After that, they spend much less to mass-produce and sell these products repeatedly over time.

Money or Time?

To apply Law Fourteen (Create Once; Sell Forever), you must reassess how you think about time and money.

If you trade your time for money, you'll never get rich. That's because your money will always be as limited as your time is. Even the brightest and the hardest working people on the planet only have twenty-four hours in a day.

Many people who aspire to be wealthy focus on creating more value to earn more. While this is an improvement over the simple time-for-money equation, it's more effective to think in terms of scale. So, while your first question might be, "How can I add value?" your follow-up should be, "How can I add value repeatedly without time being the limiting factor?"

Most people create products they can't sell repeatedly without sacrificing their time, but wealth-building enterprises like Pfizer, Salesforce, and MasterClass create products that can be sold infinitely.

What Will *You* Create?

Creating products that only result in one-time transactions is a waste of effort—anyone can sell a product once. Instead, aim to develop lasting assets that generate continuous returns. Focus on building something that will provide ongoing value and revenue long after its creation.

In other words, what can you create once that you can sell 100 times, 1,000 times, or 1 million times? The world is full of opportunities, but you have to put in the work to identify, leverage, and maximize them. Remember: The greatest leverage often stems from solutions to the simplest problems.

If you're in sales and marketing, there are so many ways to apply *create once; sell forever.*

A great way is to set up *affiliate partnerships.* As discussed in previous laws, if you frequently connect your clients with other companies, make sure that you're negotiating an affiliate commission so you get paid on every transaction. I've successfully charged 10 to 20 percent affiliate commission in a wide variety of fields adjacent to my field of expertise. If you can't get an affiliate deal, either find another person to send business to *or* try negotiating free service for yourself (in exchange for your referrals).

Another method is to create an offer and position it as an *action-taker bonus* on top of the services you're already selling. When I know the answer to someone's problem, I create a digital solution worth thousands of dollars to the client and gladly give it away as an *action-taker bonus* if they purchase on the spot. For example, if I were selling business consulting services, I could put all my email marketing templates in one place, name it something memorable like Nate's Hundred-Thousand-Dollar Email Sequence, and use it to close same-day deals.

The idea behind this is to give your clients a ton of value and save yourself thousands of dollars of your time on pointless follow-ups. This one tool helps me close an estimated $300K to $600K of additional revenue each year.

There are many ways to create additional scalable income streams. Just a heads-up—if you're a corporate employee, do this in a way that your employer wins too. If you work for a motivated leader, this shouldn't be a problem. I've successfully created several new revenue streams for my employers, and they go for it because it's in *their* best interest. If your idea attracts more customers, increases the *lifetime value* of existing customers, or creates raving fans of the brand, I bet your employer will support your efforts to create leverage for you and the company.

Best of all, you should be able to start implementing your idea immediately. In the industrial age, wealth creators needed thousands of employees to run their factories and mills. Today, the smallest teams can serve millions of consumers. Think about PayPal, Instagram, Snapchat, Evernote, Dropbox, Kickstarter, Pinterest, Spotify, and Square—and think about the size of their teams. In 2015, WhatsApp supported its massive base of 900 million active users with a team of just 50 engineers, with each engineer essentially supporting 18 million users.[53] And with the development of AI, team sizes could shrink even further. Programs like ChatGPT could soon do the work of a team of research analysts or writers. You don't need a big team for massive reach, massive impact, millions of customers, or billions in revenue.

Create once; sell forever offers tremendous opportunities for writers, artists, musicians, and other creators. In the past, an artist's output was limited to what they could produce by hand or perform live. Today, digital platforms allow creative workers to scale far beyond their original creation.

For example, a live concert reaches only those who are present. But if it is recorded and distributed on platforms like Spotify, Apple Music, or YouTube, millions can experience it, generating revenue with each play. As I write this book, I'm adding one more to the billion-plus plays of Taylor Swift's song "Style." She created it in 2014 and has been earning royalties ever since. Similarly, novelists can sell their stories multiple times through different forms, like physical books, ebooks, audiobooks, and movies.

Illustrators can sell their digital artwork repeatedly on marketplaces like Etsy, Amazon, or Shutterstock without any additional effort. Platforms like Patreon also allow artists to build a subscriber base by offering exclusive content in exchange for monthly support.

The ability to create once and sell forever is changing the way artists approach their craft. It opens new avenues for financial independence and artistic freedom, allowing creators to focus on what they love while reaching a wider audience than ever before.

On a parting note, I'd like to highlight the transformative potential of NFTs. Just as the Internet revolutionized our world, Web3 and similar technologies are positioned to do the same. NFTs enable creators to sell and resell their work on an unprecedented scale. For example, consider the Bored Ape Yacht Club, a collection of 10,000 monkey-themed artworks that generated over $1 billion in sales in just a few years.[54] While that may have been a lucky fluke, the way I see it, people are actively creating solutions to help creators make a living off of their art. Smart contracts and inventions (that come after thousands of iterations) will scale creativity and wealth creation in ways we can't imagine.

For now, the lesson is simple. Find ways to *create once and sell forever*.

Reality Check:

What million-dollar scalable asset are you sitting on?

Regardless of your current profession, you probably have a hyper-scalable business idea sitting right under your nose.

To spark your creativity, here are some real-world examples of how professionals can apply Law Fourteen:

A commercial real estate investor could sell contract templates to would-be investors. Even if they only charge a few hundred dollars for it, it's an extra drip of income they're not trading time for. Plus, there's a good chance that some of their template buyers will end up investing with them. This would give the commercial real estate investor an infinitely scalable income drip that would double as a customer acquisition tool.

A real estate agent could create and sell a video mini-course for homeowners, walking them through what to fix and what to ignore when selling their home. This could prove to be a desirable asset for the real estate agent; it's extra income, a very useful credibility tool, and a lead magnet with discount links to local contractors, all of which can be used for customer acquisition when the buyer or seller is ready to hire an agent. Additionally, this tool could also generate affiliate income from contractors, so the real estate agent gets paid when their home sellers hire a contractor to improve their home.

Again, the real estate agent creates the mini-course once, and uses it to generate multiple streams of income that generate revenue independently of their time.

A marketer could sell the email templates they're already using. They could create a bundle of email sequences once and either sell it thousands of times online or use it as an upsell to their current customers. Fellow marketers who buy these bundles would be saving hundreds of hours of their own time.

Here's another example: A graphic designer, whether freelance or employed, could use the knowledge and experience of their day job to create templates for websites, brochures, and business cards they could sell on the side.

Every profession has applications for scalable assets. Take what you've got and leverage it.

Leveraged Action Steps

This section will help you find valuable content in your job and turn it into products you can build once and sell forever.

	Leveraged Action Steps	Your Notes
#1	**System Evaluation:** Identify the systems that make your job easier and help you achieve results faster. What processes or tools do you use?	
#2	**Template Inventory:** List the templates you currently use. Examples include email templates, contracts, ROI calculators, flow charts, and marketing assets.	
#3	**Product Creation:** Sell your specialized knowledge by compiling them into a course, tool, or template.	

Chapter Fourteen Takeaway

LAW FOURTEEN
CREATE SCALABLE PRODUCTS THAT
CAN BE SOLD INFINITELY.

Don't Do Things You Hate

**"Whosoever loves much performs much,
and can accomplish much,
and what is done in love is well done."**

—Vincent Van Gogh (artist)

Stephen King, who would eventually write the legendary novel, *The Shining*, once said, "By the time I was fourteen, the nail in my wall would no longer support the weight of the rejection slips I impaled on it. I replaced the nail with a spike and went on writing."[55]

But we don't know King for his rejection letters—we know him for his successes. This just goes to show that the world will only see your victories, not the relentless effort behind them.

Today, King's horror stories are stocked in bookstores and airports everywhere. He's one of the world's best-known authors, with books that have sold more than *350 million* copies.

The King of Horror's success began with his book, *Carrie*. King created the setting for his first novel by drawing inspiration from his experiences as a high school janitor and his readings about the psychic abilities some girls exhibit at the onset of puberty. *Carrie* had an initial print run of only 30,000 copies, but it marked the beginning of a remarkable career. Since then, he has written over sixty books, becoming one of the world's richest authors with a net worth of around $500 million.[56]

In his memoir, *On Writing*, King shares his story and insights into his work, providing numerous examples of how his love and obsession for writing has shaped his work and contributed to his massive success.

King has a famously disciplined writing routine, often citing the importance of writing two thousand words every day. He believes in the routine to keep the creative juices flowing and to maintain a strong connection to the narrative thread of his works. This discipline—even through so many rejections and setbacks—has allowed him to produce an extensive body of work relatively quickly.

After a near-fatal accident in 1999, King considered retiring from writing. However, writing became a crucial part of his recovery process. He adjusted his writing routine and setup, demonstrating his dedication to his craft even during physically challenging times. This period resulted in the completion of several novels that likely would not have existed without his determination.

These are *not* the actions of a man working out of obligation or a man in it for the money or public affirmation. This is a man who loves and is *obsessed* with his craft!

The fifteenth law of leverage for building wealth is to simply *do what you love.*

To build serious wealth, you need focus and skill—and both come a lot easier if you truly enjoy what you do.

While success won't come effortlessly, the journey becomes far more manageable when you're passionate about your work. Initially, you may have to do things you hate to develop the skills and resources you need to move up. But once you've laid your foundation, *don't do things you hate.* Find work you love in a field you can dominate. Use your talents to constantly improve your work, and use your position and wealth to hire people with different skills and passions to handle the tasks you hate.

Be Obsessed or Be Irrelevant

Imagine two runners at the starting blocks, hearts pounding in anticipation of the pistol shot that will unleash their Olympic dreams. One is consumed by an unyielding love of the art of running by an obsession to cross the finish line first. Every fiber of their being is coiled for victory. The other is just happy to be part of the spectacle, content to run regardless of the outcome. In that split second before the starting pistol fires, it's clear who has the leverage—it's the runner with the most obsession. Amid any competition, obsession becomes leverage, and extraordinary effort leaves average in the dust. Hating what you do only makes the task more laborious.

There's undeniable power in an obsession that is properly harnessed—it propels you forward with a momentum that casual participation can never match. There is a time and place for casual participation, but it doesn't produce the results that obsession does.

Obsession, even in the context of the sports world, isn't just about the physical grind. It's as much about the mental and emotional focus as it is about channeling every ounce of energy in a clear direction. Obsession gets you up before dawn, hitting the pavement with muscles screaming and lungs burning, fueled by the vision of the finish line tape breaking across your chest. It's the hard work and the *heart* working together, every beat pulsing with a clear purpose. All in all, it's about love.

What Obsession is Not

With all that said, it's still very easy to get the concept of obsession wrong, so here's some clarification for you.

Obsessing over a goal is not about glorifying workaholism or suggesting that you have to grind yourself into the ground to succeed. Quite the opposite. It's about recognizing that you have to love what you're doing to become truly extraordinary.

It's not about working yourself to the bone; it's about finding work that is so aligned with your core that it barely feels like work.

When you love what you do, find purpose in your victories, and see your work as deeply meaningful, you won't settle for just "good enough." Your obsession gives you the kind of leverage that can catapult you into the top 1 percent, where excellence is commonplace. I believe that everyone needs to find meaningful work that makes the world a better place. When you become obsessed with your work, you're no longer just competing in the marketplace; you're setting the pace, defining the standards, and capturing the hearts of the world.

Don't confuse obsession with blind compulsion. It's often that quiet voice in the middle of the night telling you to try again. Obsession is the most powerful form of intrinsic motivation, which is critical for massive success.

You Won't Get Far Doing Things You Hate

On average, we spend about eight hours a day at work. While some may work fewer hours and others twice as much, most of us dedicate at least a third of our lives to our jobs.

If that work isn't fulfilling or satisfying, it *will* affect the overall quality of our lives.

If we're stuck doing what we hate (or feel stuck even when we're not), there are consequences beyond what we can immediately foresee. Yes, quitting can be scary, and it might push us out of our comfort zone, but here's the reality:

Work we don't enjoy will slowly kill us.

We stay in the grind because we've been told it's necessary. Our focus is on the financial reward at the end of the workweek. Our minds can't let go of the months and years we've already invested in our current position. We know that work is supposed to be hard, so we don't take the time to differentiate between *challenging* and *soul-crushing*.

As time goes on, finding the motivation to be productive becomes increasingly difficult. It's nearly impossible to create and innovate when you despise what you do.

You may tell yourself that the job you hate is necessary, but you're sacrificing your mental and emotional well-being in the process. At best, you won't grow. At worst, you become bored and stressed out. Even if you're in it for the money, hating your job kills your desire to develop further. This negative spiral doesn't stop at work; it spills into the rest of your life and affects your relationships with family and friends.

Unhappiness, if not contained at the source, can take over other aspects of your life.

Do what you must at the beginning. But once you are in a position to do so, leave the work you hate behind. Remember, you can't be obsessed with things you hate.

Too many people stay where they are when they could be pursuing something worth obsessing about.

Your willpower and time are limited commodities, so there's really no other way than to delegate, automate, eliminate—do whatever it takes to clear your plate for the main course: your obsessions.

When you invest your energy and time in your passions, you're running on a track made of springs. When your days are full of the work that ignites you, your need for willpower becomes obsolete, because the line between pleasure and effort blurs into insignificance. That's when you know you've transcended the average and are headed in the right direction.

Obsession in Action

Don't do things you hate isn't just a catchy phrase; it's the dividing line that separates market leaders from the pack.

Consider the tale of two tech startups. Startup A is driven by founders who live and breathe code. Their obsession with innovation has them iterating on product features before their first cup of coffee has cooled. Startup B, meanwhile, is in it to cash in on a booming market. They clock in and clock out, sticking to the roadmap without detour.

Within a year, Startup A is consistently disrupting the scene with one breakthrough after another. Startup B, meanwhile, is still tweaking its initial release. The difference? Obsession. Startup A is in a perpetual state of flow; its obsession drives innovation that leaves its competitors scrambling to try and keep up.

An obsessed company will always prevail because it's an extension of its creators' passions.

Its customer service isn't just about solving problems; it's about delighting and surprising. Its team works like they're on a mission. They aren't just clocking in hours; they're answering a calling. For an obsessed business, every piece of the puzzle is an opportunity to be remarkable, so it operates on a whole different level.

In contrast, average companies may enjoy temporary success and recognition, but they lack the magnetic pull of an obsessed culture. Without the heartbeat of passion, their efforts will be faint and forgotten. In the words of Naval Ravikant, "Do what feels like play to you, but looks like work to others."

It Adds Up

Elon Musk had a deep passion for pushing the boundaries of technology, space exploration, and renewable energy long before founding SpaceX or becoming the public face of Tesla. It took Oprah decades to become an expert interviewer. It takes a lot of time and energy to become an expert at anything, so why not do what you love on your path to success?

Mastery opens up more opportunities: higher paying jobs, expansions for entrepreneurial ventures, and better partners to light the way. With that, you can actually bring something unique to the world with your creativity. You automatically set yourself apart and become a magnet for opportunity. Steve Jobs was passionate about creating easy-to-use, beautiful technology products, which is the essence of Apple. Think about Serena Williams or Roger Federer. Without a long-term commitment, it's just not possible to be that good at anything. When you love what you do, it shows—you almost radiate that love.

The author Simon Sinek says, "People don't buy what you do—they buy why you do it." Whether you love or hate what you do really does make all the difference. It will shape your networking and relationships. It will show up in everything you say and the way you behave.

Your opportunities for wealth can either expand exponentially or shrink to nothing—depending on whether you love or hate what you do.

I'm not delusional, and I understand that not all of us have the immediate luxury of jumping into work we love. I spent several years doing meaningless grunt work that didn't make the world a better place, and I know most people have to endure the same. But over time, we can and must choose to consciously move, step by step, into work we love by finding small ways to align ourselves with our true interests and strengths.

Winning is fun, so *don't do things you hate*!

Stop Chasing Crappy Prospects

This is also why it's important to become so good at what you do that you can say no to high-maintenance clients who drain your energy. It's also a great place to start using some of the other laws of leverage too. If you're in sales or running a business, you know the customers who consume your time and complain every step of the way.

So many companies give the best deals to their worst customers. Here's how that unfolds. You take on a high-maintenance customer because you need the revenue, knowing they'll be hard to please. Then they treat your team poorly, complain that they *didn't get what they paid for*, and demand a refund. Your knee-jerk reaction might be to go above and beyond to keep them happy, so you end up doing twice the work for half the pay. Well, that's not a good solution.

What if you stopped serving everyone who wants your help? What if you got a little picky and only worked with the top 90 percent of people who approached you? That is still the majority, and the world has more clients to offer than you could ever hope to serve. So leave the bottom 10 percent of clientele to someone else and spend that time finding more people in the 90 percent. This could mean eliminating the client from your list altogether. It could also mean using OPT and giving the bottom 10 percent to someone else.

Over the years, I've mastered the art of referring unwanted business to other companies. As soon as I hear complaints like, "Why should I choose you over the competition?", "Why are your prices so high?", or "What can you do for free?", I either take control of the conversation or politely refer them elsewhere.

This saves me from work I hate and allows me to focus on clients who truly value my services. Not only do I enjoy my work more, but my chosen clients get better results and I become more profitable. So once you have credibility, stop chasing crappy prospects and crappy partnerships. Instead, save your best offers for your best customers who value your work and are most likely to refer more business to you.

Reality Check

Do you love what you do?

This may be shocking, but I enjoy my work more than I enjoy sitting on a sandy white beach at an all-inclusive resort in Cancun or taking a six-week vacation in Europe. I enjoy those things, but I enjoy work more.

Now, before you start thinking that my priorities are out of whack, let me explain why I love work more than most:

- The work I do is deeply meaningful to me.

- I make the world a better place through my work.

- I feel accomplished when I'm learning, growing, and winning at new levels.

- I'm addicted to winning! I've doubled my income every year for the past four years, and it feels incredible.

Do you have a similar relationship with your work?

Do you love what you do?

Part of the reason some people love work and others think that idea is crazy is because we have different definitions of work.

"Work" is something I get the privilege of doing. For some people, work is something they have to do. If work is painful to you, you will find any excuse to avoid it. But when you love what you do, work is something you look forward to.

Roughly 50 percent of the people in the world don't like their jobs, and I'm going to make an educated guess that a large portion of the remaining 50 percent would like to do something else if they were in a financial position to do so. So those who really love their work are in the minority.

Most people spend forty-plus hours a week doing things they don't like. And the sad part is they probably won't win big because they'll lose to an obsessed player who actually enjoys the tasks at hand.

Leveraged Action Steps

Have you identified your passion in life, and are you using your obsession as leverage to build wealth? If you are not, consider the following:

	Leveraged Action Steps	Your Notes
#1	**Identify Passion Activities:** What activities could you do forever without getting bored?	
#2	**Skill Set Utilization:** What jobs utilize some form of that skill set?	
#3	**Self-Driven Learning:** What knowledge or skills do you pursue without being asked to?	
#4	**Streamline Your Role:** Identify the parts of your job you don't love and then delegate, automate, and eliminate. Do whatever it takes to clear your plate for the main course: your obsessions.	

Chapter Fifteen Takeaway

LAW FIFTEEN
DON'T DO THINGS YOU HATE. FIND WORK THAT
ALLOWS YOU TO THRIVE AND DOMINATE.

Don't Work for Money

**"True wealth is measured by your ability to
sustain your lifestyle without having to work."**

—Unknown

In a world captivated by high salaries and lavish lifestyles, there's a pervasive and misleading illusion that a fat paycheck equates to real wealth.

It's a trap that countless people unwittingly fall into, measuring their success by the numbers on their monthly income statements, when the real dynamics of wealth look very different.

High salaries and corporate perks provide immediate gratification. They may also be temporarily necessary to build up capital. But real wealth—the kind that provides lasting freedom and prosperity—goes way beyond the immediate dollars that hit your bank account at the end of the month. True financial wealth comes from the accumulation of assets and resources that not only support your lifestyle through regular cash flows but also grow and multiply over time.

This leads us to an indispensable concept in the realm of wealth and our next law of leverage: The wealthy don't work for money. Remember, *leverage* is about using minimal effort to achieve maximum returns. While those who seek wealth through a salary *work harder* to increase their income, the wealthy strategically position their resources to work for them.

Would you rather chase money or let money chase you?

The Wealthy Don't Work for Money; They Have Money Work for Them

Think about it: How many wealthy people do you know who work a hard nine-to-five, trading their precious hours for dollars?

Making your money work for you isn't just a catchy phrase. It's a different way of thinking about wealth—and one that pays off handsomely when you get it right. Flip the script and make your money work for you, so you don't have to toil for it.

The big question is, how will you do that?

You may have heard of *passive* cash flow. It's a way to make your money work for you. Building passive cash flow streams is like having a golden goose in your backyard; instead of working for every dime, you're collecting the golden eggs that are laid while you sleep, play, or work on your next big thing. When done right, passive income requires minimal to no effort to maintain. It's the rental income from a property you own, the dividends from your stocks, or the royalties from a book or song you wrote years ago.

Now, passive income doesn't mean no work at all—it often requires significant upfront effort or capital. But once established, the ongoing demands diminish, and the rewards keep coming. It's like planting a tree. You put in the hard work initially and water it diligently, but in time, the tree will stand tall and bear fruit every year without much fuss—that's passive cash flow.

Why Passive Income Beats Earned Income

Let's say you meet a genie who offers you a choice that will determine your financial future.

Option 1: Receive an annual salary of $850K for the rest of your life. This would provide you with a luxurious lifestyle and all the trappings of success, but you'd have to work very hard every day.

Option 2: Receive $100K a year in passive income without working a single day for it. The money comes into your bank account, year after year, no matter where you are or what you're doing.

Most people choose Option 1 because the higher amount seems like the obvious choice. But it's not that simple. Choosing the $850K salary binds you; it must be earned year after year, and it tethers you to the demands that salary places on your time, energy, and values. Choosing the $100K in passive income, though significantly less, offers a different kind of wealth—the wealth of freedom.

When you choose freedom, your time becomes entirely your own, which is a wealth of opportunity that no salary can match. When you're not stuck in a demanding job where you feel like someone "owns" you, you have more energy, more time, and a more positive attitude. You can travel, pursue hobbies, spend time with loved ones, create more income streams, invest in personal growth, or simply enjoy the day as it unfolds. Whenever possible, choose time freedom over income. If you control your time, you can control your income.

The benefits are greater than you might think. Consider the tax implications. Earned income is taxed at a higher rate than passive income, which can be sheltered through various tax vehicles. (We'll talk about this in more detail in the next chapter.) So while the $850K is impressive, the take-home pay is significantly less after the taxman takes his cut. On the other hand, that $100K of passive income can often be sheltered to retain a higher percentage of its value.

Second, the security of passive income can be more robust than that of a high-paying job. Once upon a time, perhaps as far back as the twentieth century, one of the biggest drivers of work was *job security*. Employment with a company typically lasted several decades, subsequent pensions meant steady growth, and for the most part, employers and employees stuck together to the end. All you have to do is open a newspaper to see that today's work environment is very different, with economic downturns and unexpected events causing layoffs at a moment's notice. Now it seems that passive income sources weather economic storms better and provide a more stable financial foundation.

Finally, if you still want to actively work very hard to create more wealth (i.e., bridge the gap between $100K and $850K—or perhaps even aim much higher), nothing and no one is stopping you. The difference is that you'll be working hard *because you want to*, not because *you have to*. Just look at Warren Buffett. He loves his work so much that he says he "tap dances to work every morning." He doesn't need the money, but he works because he loves it. His advice to recent graduates is to "take the job you would take if you were independently wealthy," because it's about following your passion and letting the money follow you.[57]

A high-earning income gives you instant gratification and status. Passive income will give you longevity, stability, and time freedom—which may also result in greater financial freedom as well.

Now look at the genie's offer again and choose wisely.

Building Wealth Through Ownership

Imagine you could be the captain of one of two vastly different seagoing vessels: A single-person rowboat and a diesel-powered freighter.

In the rowboat, you're alone in the choppy waters of the sea. Every mile forward is won by the sweat of your brow and the strength of your arms. You toil daily against the currents, trading your precious time and energy for each hard-earned mile. The moment your oars lift from the water, the vessel falters, and the rapids of recurring bills threaten to drag you back to where you started.

Now imagine yourself at the helm of a colossal diesel freighter. This ship doesn't rely on your physical strength; it's driven by powerful engines—your investments and holdings. On this ship, your wealth isn't dependent on your effort or presence; it's generated by the mighty engines below deck. You're no longer a row master toiling for a paycheck. Instead, you're a strategic navigator commanding a formidable fleet of wealth-generating machines.

This law of leverage is to help you transition from mastering the first boat to the second one—so, let's look at some practical ways to jump into a better ship.

1. Buy a Business: This isn't about being the boss; it's about owning a stake in a revenue-generating system. One of the best ways to do this is to buy an already established business with the intention of never becoming the boss. Being the boss and managing the headaches sucks. Owning the revenue stream is the goal.

2. Own Real Estate Investments: Owning real estate is a classic path to wealth for a reason. Whether you own residential, commercial, or apartment buildings, or buy into syndicated real estate deals that don't require your time and effort, you can generate large amounts of income from rent and capital appreciation. We'll discuss the practical steps for buying syndicated real estate in Law Seventeen.

3. Own Intellectual Property (Trademarks/Copyrights): This is the realm of authors, artists, and inventors. When you own intellectual property, such as copyrights to books or trademarks, you earn royalties on every sale or use. Even the smallest monthly income makes a massive difference over a decade.

4. Own Insurance Books of Business: It's rarely discussed, but you can buy business books from insurance agents and brokers. You pay them up front and collect the premiums as long as the client pays their life insurance, annuity, etc. It's like buying a money tree.

Syndicated real estate, trademarks, copyrights, and insurance books of business are my personal favorite forms of recurring revenue. I never think about them, and they pay me every single month. These compound over time and create a constant stream of income that I reinvest and spend as needed.

These options, and so many more, are a means of charting your way out of the choppy waters of wage earning and into the safe harbor of passive income. Master these strategies, and you'll command a fleet of income streams that build upon each other over time, ensuring that you'll never have to live paycheck to paycheck again.

"Pay me in Equity"

Beyoncé's famous song lyric, "Pay me in equity," encapsulates a great deal of financial acumen for lasting wealth in just four words.

When someone asks for compensation in the form of equity, they're demonstrating that they understand the limitations of liquid cash and are willing to forgo it in favor of the expansive potential of ownership. There are success stories throughout history and into the modern era of people who shifted their focus from income to long-term equity.

Soccer player Lionel Messi is a great example. Messi turned down a three-year, *$1.6 billion offer*[58] for an equity stake in Inter Miami. Had Messi opted to join Al-Hilal in Saudi Arabia after parting ways with Paris Saint-Germain, the world's most famous soccer player would have been significantly richer (in the short term). Messi turned down the *$1.6 billion payday* for equity in the Inter Miami club, with percentages of earnings in its merchandise deals with Apple and Adidas. By choosing equity over a paycheck, Messi prioritized his family's earnings over the long haul in ways he couldn't have with a more traditional payment structure. This choice positioned him for long-term financial gains beyond his playing years. By choosing equity, Messi chose freedom.

Athletes, in particular, face unique challenges regarding career longevity. Unlike many professions where people can work into their sixties or beyond, athletes often retire in their thirties because of the physical demands of their sport. This reality makes investments and equity stakes a prudent and necessary long-term strategy. Understanding that their sports contracts have a finite lifespan, many athletes make these strategic decisions early in life to ensure financial stability long after their athletic careers end. By converting their temporary high earnings into perpetual equity, they secure their financial future and often create substantial wealth.

Another celebrity who translated his fame into ownership is LeBron James, who invested his basketball earnings in numerous business ventures, including becoming a part-owner of Liverpool Football Club through a partnership with Fenway Sports Group.[52]

Rihanna traded her earnings to invest in Fenty Beauty, again demonstrating the power of channeling brand influence into a stake in a $1 billion company.

This is not just for celebrities. Many of the early employees of Facebook and Google became millionaires when the companies went public. All of these stories have a common thread: the individuals involved recognized the limitations of earned income and chose the liberating potential of passive income and equity. The message is clear: Look beyond the paycheck. Seek out equity opportunities that align with your skills, interests, and financial goals, and plant seeds that will grow into fruitful income trees.

A mindset shift toward equity is crucial for anyone transitioning from high income to sustainable wealth. Equity, simply put, is ownership, so it's not a direct exchange of time for money. Instead, it's the leveraging of capital or intellectual contribution to gain a share of future profits.

Building wealth is not without risk, but the "pay me in equity" philosophy embraces that risk in exchange for more substantial and lasting rewards. So play the long game and build equity so your family can benefit from today's efforts forever.

Fool's Gold

I have a friend who makes $1.2 million a year in sales commissions selling paint to commercial contractors. His manager has a more prestigious title but makes one-fifth of that. To the outside world, the manager appears to be more successful, but their bank statements tell a different story. Moreover, the salesman has the mobility and capital to acquire more assets, allowing him to exponentially outpace and outmaneuver the manager.

Over time, I expect this income gap to widen as my friend applies his skills to new ventures. With each sale he makes, he becomes an even better salesman and builds the network he needs to pivot in the future. Not only does he outearn his manager, but he also has a better leverage point for his next exponential move.

So don't get so caught up in climbing the ladder of perceived success that you end up on the *wrong* ladder. Not every promotion will get you closer to your goals. Be wary of promotions that offer status but stifle your progress.

A key component to getting out of the rat race is simply not giving up on trying to get out of the rat race. Remember, you're not just creating wealth for today; you're building wealth for a lifetime and generations to come. It takes vision, patience, and persistence. The road to lasting wealth is not linear; it's paved with trials, errors, and triumphs.

Just don't give up. It's not easy, but it is that simple. Keep going, even when it's hard. One of my favorite inspirational clips of all time is Alex Hormozi's take on what it feels like to fail your way to success: "It's painful ... because the whole time, everyone is telling you, 'I told you so,' and they're right ... today ... but not forever."

The pain you go through today to escape the rat race will be worth it when you succeed at living life on your own terms. When that day comes, you will look back and smile at how far you've come.

Reality Check

Are you building wealth or just earning a paycheck?

In today's fast-paced world, it's easy to put all your energy into your job, leaving little time to build your family's equity. But true wealth comes from building things that pay you forever. Here's how to start shifting your focus.

Paycheck Versus Equity:

Take a moment to review your work over the past month. How much of your time resulted in a one-time paycheck, and how much contributed to long-term equity?

Pick one strategy from this chapter that speaks to you—whether it's investing in real estate, buying a small business, or developing a passive income stream.

Focus on that single idea and take actionable steps to move it forward. For example, if you're interested in real estate, hire someone to help you buy your first property.

Prioritize your best hours: Dedicate the first few hours of your day to wealth-building activities. Spend your peak productivity hours on wealth-building projects before you dive into your regular job responsibilities. This approach will yield more significant results over time than any other daily task your job has you complete.

Shift your focus gradually by trading a few hours of "paycheck" work for "equity" work. If you normally work forty hours a week, start by reallocating a few of those hours to your wealth-building activities. This could include researching investments, developing a side hustle, or taking an online course to improve your skills. Over time, these small shifts will compound to significant financial growth.

By gradually shifting some of your most focused hours to wealth-building activities, you're leveraging your time to ensure that you and your family will reap the benefits for years to come.

Leveraged Action Steps

Review your calendar from last month. How much of your work resulted in a paycheck, and how much built equity?

Time Spent on Paycheck	Time Spent Building Equity

Chapter Sixteen Takeaway

LAW SIXTEEN
DON'T WORK FOR MONEY; POSITION
YOURSELF SO THAT MONEY CHASES YOU.

Don't Own Anything on Paper

**"The secret to success is to own
nothing but control everything."**

—Nelson Rockefeller (American businessman
and grandson of John D. Rockefeller)

As I write this book, Tesla's stock is at a four-month high, and Elon Musk's net worth is $207 billion.[60] And yet, on paper, he owns virtually nothing personally. Musk's business holdings, houses, cars, and so on are all owned by his LLCs (or limited liability companies) and corporate entities.[61]

When Nelson Rockefeller said, "The secret to success is to own nothing but control everything," he was referring to asset protection. Owning nothing on paper in your own name is a way of gaining leverage to protect your wealth. Most of the ultra-wealthy use legal entities, such as LLCs, to hold assets because it can protect you in at least four ways: it limits your liability, reduces your tax burden, helps with privacy, and preserves wealth for generations.

When a business structure owns assets on paper, rather than an individual, it legally separates those assets from the individual owner. This means that in the event of a lawsuit, liability, or pursuing creditor, the owners typically cannot be held personally liable. People generally use one of two types of legal entities: S corporations and LLCs. While the latter is usually preferred because it is more flexible, both offer tax benefits and protections to their owners.[62] Using a corporate mechanism for ownership also helps save taxes because owning assets through a corporation allows expenses to be deducted as business expenses and often offers more favorable corporate tax rates. Owners may also be able to defer paying taxes on the profits of the business until those profits are distributed as dividends. Next, layering trusts with LLCs helps keep the owner (and what they own) private, which can be important from a security standpoint. And lastly, using an entity to hold assets simplifies the transfer of ownership in succession planning when it comes time to transfer assets to heirs or other parties, while simultaneously protecting those assets from additional taxes that might apply to such transfers.

The seventeenth law of leverage is simple. If you want to preserve and compound your wealth, don't own anything on paper; use corporate entities to your advantage instead.

It's Not About How Much You Earn; It's About How Much You Keep

Grant Cardone says, "The goal of the wealthy is to earn *no* income. That's because earning no income also means *paying no taxes.*"[63]

Amazon's Jeff Bezos is a fantastic example. In 2007, Bezos added $3.8 billion to his wealth but paid no federal income tax. He offset his

$46 million of reported income with paper losses from investments, expenses, and debt-related deductions. He also paid no income tax the following year, according to the same source. Even in recent years, he's seen his fortune soar. His net worth grew by *$99 billion* in the four years between 2014 and 2018, but he only paid a true tax rate of 0.98 percent (less than 1 percent).[64]

The wealth he's created is impressive, but the fact that he's kept *almost all of it* is even more impressive.

That's the power of using the LLC as leverage.

LLCs help shelter a significant amount of your income from taxes and are not very difficult to form. When money is earned through a corporation, the corporation covers the expenses. This may seem like the same thing as a person earning income and covering expenses, but the key difference is *when* you are taxed on the income that is earned.

A corporation will make money, cover expenses first, and *then* pay taxes on what is left. A person will make money, *pay taxes first*, and *then* cover expenses from their post-tax income.[65] And it's only when you add up the pieces that you can properly estimate how much extra you'll pay in taxes if you don't use entities like LLCs.

Take the case of Warren Buffett, a longtime fan of Coca-Cola. His firm invested in Coke stock in 1988, in part because Buffett himself loved the beverage. In an annual letter, Buffett said, "When we own parts of outstanding companies with outstanding managements, our favorite holding period is *forever*." True to his word, the investment has appreciated 2,232.7 percent over the past thirty-three years, for an average annual return of around 68 percent.

In February 2015, when Coca-Cola's stock rose 3 percent, Buffett made $508 million as an investor, while Coca-Cola's CEO made $25.2 million running the company the previous year.[66, 67] Not only did Buffett make significantly more, but his company also paid a lower tax rate on the capital gains compared to the CEO's earned income. This is because passive income is taxed at a lower rate than earned income, especially if you have a competent tax planner on your team.

Buffett highlighted this disparity by noting that his employees paid an average tax rate of 32.9 percent, while he paid only 17.7 percent because his wealth came primarily from capital gains. Despite being one of the richest people in the world, he benefits from lower taxes because of the way his income is structured.[68]

Another important benefit of investment income is that it often avoids the additional burden of payroll taxes. Investors who earn passive K-1 income through partnerships or LLCs generally do not pay FICA or SECA taxes, which fund Social Security and Medicare.[69] By earning income as an investor rather than as an employee or self-employed individual, you can further reduce the tax bite, allowing more of your money to work for you, compound and grow over time.

And let's face it, you'll find ways to earn a much higher rate of return than your Social Security check could ever pay you in the future.

This situation underscores a broader point: Investors and owners often take home more in profits and pay less in taxes than the boss. Investment income, such as dividends or long-term capital gains, is taxed at lower rates than ordinary income. In the U.S., the tax system has seven brackets ranging from 10 percent to 37 percent, with the most successful people paying the highest rates. As income increases, so does the tax rate, which can be discouraging for those who contribute the most to society.

Think about that for a moment.

So many people want to be the boss, but the boss has to deal with the headaches, the long hours, and the higher taxes, while investors avoid the headaches, earn higher profits, and pay lower taxes. I recommend choosing the easier, more profitable path.

Don't be the boss; be the investor.

Forget about earned income. To win the wealth game, you need to be the investor in the business, not the manager. You must own assets through *the right vehicles* and learn how to protect that wealth from erosion.

What Baseball Teaches Us About Taxes

Some groups of people have mastered the art of using depreciation to minimize their tax liability, and baseball team owners are one such group. Using their teams' corporate structures as leverage, billionaire team owners often pay a substantially lower tax rate than their millionaire players.

Baseball team owners make extensive use of vehicles such as player contracts, television contracts, and other tangible and intangible assets to reduce their tax liability.

Bill Veeck, a former owner of the Cleveland Indians and Chicago White Sox, developed a tax strategy that allowed team owners to claim significant tax deductions through the depreciation of player contracts. His innovation was to treat player contracts as separate, depreciable assets, distinct from the team itself. By purchasing these contracts separately, Veeck was able to allocate a large portion of a team's purchase price to the value of these contracts.[20]

Because assets like equipment and real estate can depreciate in value over time, Veeck's method allowed him to claim a tax deduction based on the perceived depreciation of the player contracts. This deduction could be used to offset the team's profits and other unrelated income. The IRS eventually approved this strategy, allowing team owners in Major League Baseball and other sports to reduce their taxes by treating player contracts as assets that lose value over time. This tax strategy gave team owners substantial financial benefits and made the business that much more lucrative.

Team owners have the advantage of being able to act like chess masters, moving pieces around to suit their interests. Here's a review of federal tax records that highlight the disparity in tax rates between owners and players, showing the preferential treatment team owners receive under the tax code compared to wage-earning athletes.

As of 2023, the average MLB player earns $4.9 million per year. However, depending on their state of residence, they might end up paying 50 to 60 percent of that in taxes and fees. This includes a 37 percent federal income tax, up to 9.65 percent state income tax, property tax, sales tax, and various other fees and licenses. After all these deductions, their impressive salary becomes significantly less so.

So, what did smart ballplayers do when they realized their team owners were paying less taxes than they were? They took the concepts their team owners used to lower their taxable income and found leverage points they could apply for themselves.

One of the ways ballplayers lower their taxable income is by investing the majority of their $4.9 million salary in multifamily and commercial real estate *before* paying taxes on it. Treat yourself like a corporation: make money, cover expenses *first*, and *then* pay taxes on what is left over. The way ballplayers accomplish this legally is by purchasing large assets and using cost segregation studies to create a *paper loss* on the $4.9 million, which they write off on their tax bill. They look broke on paper, but the reality is that they own substantial assets and live off the cash flow the properties generate.

The Role of a CPA in the Big Leagues

Once you start making upward of $300K to $400K a year, I highly recommend that you find a tax planner or CPA who specializes in real estate and high-net-worth individuals.

As with any profession, there are average CPAs and there are exceptional ones. There are CPAs who will tell you what you can and can't write off, and there are CPAs who will find a way to write off anything you give them (legally, of course). Exceptional CPAs are hard to come by, which is why building relationships with successful people can be so valuable. I found my tax planner through the wealthiest real estate professional I know. Our tax planner has been one of the most important forms of leverage my wife and I have had in recent years.

In the big leagues, a CPA isn't just a tax preparer; they're a key player on your financial team. A good tax planner can save you more in taxes than most people make.

Their secret weapon? Cost segregation studies and bonus depreciation.

A cost segregation study breaks down the purchase price of a property and assigns the various structural components to different categories based on how quickly each component would hypothetically deteriorate and require replacement. These studies are typically performed by cost segregation specialists or engineers who perform detailed analyses of properties to identify asset components that can be reclassified into shorter depreciation periods for tax purposes.[21]

Through a meticulous process, they catalog every component in the building, from the finishes and fixtures to the structure and roofing materials, and calculate the life of each component and when it's due for replacement. Then your tax planner can write-off all of your *future* renovation costs *up front* on your taxes, lowering your tax bill in the present and maximizing your tax benefits early in your investment timeline. This process is commonly known as *accelerated depreciation* or *bonus depreciation*.

Accelerated depreciation and bonus depreciation are similar concepts but differ in how deductions are applied. Accelerated depreciation includes a number of methods that increase the rate at which an asset can be depreciated, allowing for higher tax deductions in earlier years. Bonus depreciation, on the other hand, refers specifically to deducting 100 percent of the future depreciation of an asset up front, rather than spreading the deduction out over several years. Thanks to the Tax Cuts and Jobs Act of 2017, bonus depreciation allowed for a 100 percent first-year deduction on many assets, including machinery and certain real estate improvements.[22] These upfront deductions have been and will be one of the main strategies for reducing your taxable income to zero. Although bonus depreciation is slowly being phased out for traditional real estate assets, this principle is still very much alive in other asset classes, which we'll get to later.

There are two key points of leverage that make bonus depreciation so effective. The first point of leverage is that you're taking all your tax deductions decades in advance. By reinvesting the tax savings immediately, you could hopefully triple or quadruple your investment by the end of the 39-year tax period.

The second point of leverage is the debt acquired on the asset. Going back to the baseball player scenario I mentioned earlier, debt is how they write off the full $4.9 million (instead of just a portion).

Let me explain. If you bought a $4.9 million property in cash, you may only have a few million of that in depreciating components for your building. This means that you can only depreciate a portion of the $4.9 million on your taxes.

If you put $4.9 million down on a $14 million commercial property and financed the rest with a commercial loan, you'll benefit from $14 million worth of depreciating parts like countertops and microwaves, even though you only put 35 percent down. Leveraging debt is a great way to avoid paying taxes, and there are a variety of strategies that accomplish this. For example, many ultra-wealthy people choose to borrow against their stocks and investments rather than sell them because they don't pay taxes on debt, but they do pay capital gains tax when they sell their assets.

Debt is often portrayed in a negative light. While this may be true for the average credit card debt, it's a different story for millionaires and billionaires who use it as a strategic tool to lower their taxes. They understand that by leveraging debt, they can acquire more assets and use the added depreciation to lower their taxes and improve their overall position. Debt, when used wisely, can be a powerful component of an overall wealth-building strategy.

The U.S. government (and many other nations) allows real estate professionals to take these massive tax breaks up front as an incentive to motivate their citizens to build their nation's infrastructure. When these properties are eventually sold, the government will *recapture* the deferred taxable income, but you can use something called a 1031 exchange to flip that income into another real estate deal to repeat the process and delay the taxable event indefinitely.

The better you are at lowering your taxes, the more of your wealth you can preserve.

Navigating The 1031 Exchange

Selling investment property may not be the goal, but sometimes, even the most steadfast property holders need to sell.

The unpredictability of life, coupled with the whims of the market, means that even the most durable investment plans may require alterations. Maintenance burdens, changes in neighborhood dynamics, or simply a deliberate decision to invest elsewhere may dictate the sale of a property.

In these situations, the wisest investors employ a 1031 exchange—a strategy as adaptable as it is savvy. Named after Section 1031 of the U.S. Internal Revenue Code, this strategy allows investors to defer capital gains tax by reinvesting the proceeds from the sale of one investment property into a new one. It's a legitimate way of telling the IRS, "I'll pay you later."

The 1031 exchange is a powerful tool, but timing is everything. After an asset is sold, there is a period of time to identify new investment opportunities, with an additional period to complete the acquisition. When executed with precision, this exchange allows you to transfer gains from one property to another and defer payment for the taxes indefinitely. This method allows you to effectively exchange one asset for another, ensuring that your wealth is poised for continued and uninhibited growth, all within the confines of the law.[23]

The Rockefeller Method

The Rockefellers view wealth not merely as a matter of accumulation but as a family legacy, and their strategy is as solid as the bedrock of Manhattan itself.

Unlike others, they do not rush to sell properties for immediate gains. Instead, they retain their assets indefinitely, allowing them to appreciate over time while strategically leveraging the legal and tax systems to their advantage.

This approach—a meticulous game of patience and planning—has sustained the family's wealth for more than a century and a half. The compounded growth of their assets and the shrewd reduction of taxes will perpetuate the Rockefellers' prosperity well into the future.

The Rockefeller method includes a particularly effective tactic known as tax-free debt. As the value of their real estate increases, so does their equity—but the Rockefellers typically refinance rather than sell. They extract money as a loan, which is not recognized as income and, therefore, is not taxable. This turns static equity into liquid capital for reinvestment (or to support their lifestyle) without triggering a taxable event. This tactic exemplifies the Rockefeller ethos: increase liquidity while avoiding tax implications.

Another critical component of the Rockefellers' wealth preservation can be seen in their wealth transfer. When the Rockefellers pass down their assets, the basis of the assets is adjusted to their current market value at the time of inheritance. This "reset" eliminates any potential capital gains taxes that may have accumulated, effectively wiping the slate clean. The deferred taxes are wiped out, giving the heirs the assets at full market value, unencumbered by any previous tax liabilities.

This adjustment to the cost basis of inherited assets is known as a "step-up in basis" and is a powerful tax-saving tool.[74] It allows the Rockefellers to rack up a bunch of deferred taxes and then wipe the slate clean when they pass their assets on to future generations. Without this adjustment, heirs would owe taxes on decades of appreciation, slowing their financial progress. By resetting the basis to current market value, the Rockefellers ensure that future generations will benefit from the appreciation without incurring capital gains taxes.

This strategy is not unique to the Rockefellers. Step-up in basis is widely used in estate planning by wealthy families in the U.S. and other countries with similar tax systems. Many well-to-do families use it to reduce capital gains taxes and protect their wealth across generations.

Lastly, they're known for their strategic diversification of investments, which insulates the family portfolio from market volatility. They are extremely proactive in instilling financial literacy, responsibility, and philanthropy in future generations. It's ingrained in every generation of the family, which has created an unstoppable cycle of perpetual growth.

Syndicated Real Estate Investing

Imagine being part of an elite investment club where the compound interest or internal rate of return (IRR) ranges from 15 to 20 percent *and* you get massive tax breaks *and* you don't have to lift a finger. These investments accelerate your wealth-building journey by compounding your money while simultaneously reducing your taxable income. And it's not just for the ultra-wealthy; anyone who qualifies as an accredited investor can participate. Becoming an accredited investor is within reach for a lot of people who don't realize it. To qualify, you must have earned at least $200K per year (or $300K jointly with a spouse) in the last two years and expect to earn the same or more in the current year. Alternatively, you may qualify if your net worth exceeds $1 million, excluding the value of your primary residence.[25] If you don't meet either of these criteria, a competent CPA may be able to make this accessible for you with a little creative maneuvering.

Instead of letting your hard-earned cash sit in a bank account, put it into assets that appreciate over time and give you a tax break up front. (Although the strategies I present here are specific to the United States of America, many countries have similar tax deductions.)

Syndication unleashes the power of pooling resources and allows individual investors to band together and invest in properties that would be out of reach on their own. It's like getting roommates to afford a bigger apartment—you share the cost and enjoy a better place to live. This collective buying power paves the way for high-value, high-return investments. There are many real estate syndicates that pay 15 to 20 percent compound interest, so you can double your money in less than five years.

Now combine that enticing IRR with the magical tax benefits that come with these deals. Most of these deals will give you a 50 to 60 percent depreciation write-off on the portion of the asset you're buying. This gives you a paper loss that you can use to lower your current taxable income or carry forward to lower your taxes in the future. Between the compounding 15 to 20 percent and the 50 to 60 percent paper loss, you've got a winning combination. Every dollar you invest works toward earning a hefty return and acts as a shield against your current taxable income.

Let's break it down with some quick math.

A $100K investment can result in a $50K to $60K write-off up front. As mentioned earlier in this chapter, the U.S. government allows real estate investors to calculate the material components of the buildings they own and take accelerated depreciation on those material components up front. This significantly reduces your taxable income for the year, allowing you to keep more of your hard-earned money. Plus, you've strengthened your balance sheet, created an investment, and increased your cash reserves. You get the cash flow along with the equity when the property is sold. When the property is sold, the government wants to *recapture* the taxable income, but you can use a 1031 exchange to flip that income into another syndicated deal to repeat the process and further delay the tax payments.

So your $100K investment should turn into about $219,245 in five years, while giving you a $50K to $60K tax break up front to protect you from the taxman. From there, you can continue to roll that capital into future deals, increasing your profit every step of the way.

If you're a 1099 or contract employee, the path to reducing your taxable income through syndicated real estate investing is straightforward.

Accelerated depreciation from the assets can be applied directly to 1099 income, resulting in significant tax savings.

If you're a W2 employee, leveraging real estate for tax benefits might seem more challenging because of IRS regulations, which typically prevent you from offsetting W2 income with depreciation from real estate. However, there is a nuanced strategy that remains underutilized: If you or your spouse qualify as a real estate professional and spend at least 750 hours per year in real estate activities, you can use your real estate depreciation to offset your W2 wages. To qualify as a real estate professional, all you have to do is log 750 hours per year in any real estate-related activity (interior design, real estate photography, property management, research, etc.) and make sure that at least 50 percent of your work hours are spent on real estate activities.[76] Although these two requirements can be difficult to achieve as a full-time W2 employee, the IRS will let your spouse qualify for the family, which is much more feasible. That is why many spouses of high-earning individuals do some form of real estate work on the side, so that their family can benefit from the tax write-offs.

Work toward meeting these two requirements, and then let your CPA or tax planner know. There are no forms or paperwork to fill out on your taxes to qualify. Just a simple checkmark and voila! You now have a way to keep more of your hard-earned capital.

Just a quick note: This strategy, while powerful, requires compliance with IRS regulations. That's why I recommend hiring a tax professional who understands the interplay between earned income and real estate investments. Having an experienced tax professional as an active part of your wealth creation team can be incredibly useful.

If qualifying as a real estate professional would be complicated for your situation, there are many syndicated opportunities in oil, ATMs, and laundromats that do not require these qualifications. Some of these opportunities offer higher depreciation percentages and do not require the *recapture* of accelerated depreciation upon sale. This allows you to enjoy the tax benefits without the 1031 exchange on the back end.

Understanding Bonus Depreciation and its Expiration

Bonus depreciation is one of the primary tax tools that allows real estate investors to accelerate the deductions they can take on certain real estate expenses. The 2017 Tax Cuts and Jobs Act made bonus depreciation particularly attractive. Under this law, investors were able to deduct 100 percent of the cost of qualifying assets in the first year they were placed in service. Qualifying assets include things like appliances, flooring, and other components of a building that depreciate faster than the building itself. This meant that real estate investors could significantly reduce their taxable income in the first year of owning or improving a property, freeing up cash for other investments.

Bonus depreciation for traditional real estate assets is currently being phased out. Starting in 2023, the full 100 percent deduction was reduced to 80 percent, and it will continue to decrease over the coming years: 60 percent in 2024, 40 percent in 2025, and 20 percent in 2026.[22] After 2026, bonus depreciation is set to disappear entirely unless Congress enacts new legislation to extend it. Once the phase-out is complete, real estate investors will still be able to depreciate their assets, but the deduction will revert to the traditional schedules, with depreciation periods of 5, 7, or 15 years for various components, rather than allowing for full first-year deductions. While the tax benefits won't be as immediate, investors can still enjoy the long-term benefits of owning and depreciating real estate.

Now that we've explored the tax benefits of traditional real estate, it's important to note that there are plenty of other asset classes where accelerated depreciation is still in full force.

Maximizing Tax Savings with Syndicated Oil Funds

While the tax deductions for syndicated real estate investments are currently on the decline, the core principles of accelerated depreciation and depletion in oil funds remain as powerful as ever for reducing taxable income while increasing passive income.

Syndicated oil funds are a nice alternative for investors looking to diversify beyond traditional real estate assets. There are many oil opportunities that allow you to write off 80 to 100 percent of your initial investment (primarily) through Intangible Drilling Costs (IDCs), which cover intangible expenses like labor and drilling supplies.[78] For example, if you invest $100K, you could reduce your taxable income by $80K to $100K in the first year alone.

Additionally, you will benefit from the 15 percent depletion allowance once the well begins producing. This excludes 15 percent of the gross income from the well from your taxable income. This ongoing deduction increases the overall tax efficiency of these investments. Unlike depreciation, depletion can sometimes exceed 100 percent of the initial cost of investment. This is because an oil well might produce for more than 30 years which makes the cumulative tax benefits substantial.

W2 earners who *do not* qualify as real estate professionals can still use oil and gas investments to offset their ordinary income. Unlike traditional real estate assets, where depreciation is being spread out over years, oil and gas investments provide an immediate and substantial reduction in taxable income which makes them an attractive option for high-income earners.

Another key advantage of syndicated oil funds is that the IRS does not recapture accelerated depreciation on these investments. This sets them apart from real estate assets where depreciation is often recaptured and taxed upon sale. Syndicated oil funds don't have that requirement so you won't need a 1031 exchange to defer taxes, giving you more flexibility and simplicity in managing your investment.

While syndicated real estate funds often get the spotlight, many syndicated oil funds offer much higher returns and much better tax incentives. The combination of accelerated tax depreciation through IDCs, ongoing depletion allowances, and the absence of depreciation recapture makes this a powerful strategy for growing wealth while minimizing taxes.

Maximizing Tax Benefits with Syndicated ATM Funds

If oil funds aren't your preferred investment, syndicated ATM funds offer another compelling option that is available to non-real-estate professionals. These investments allow you to take advantage of accelerated depreciation, allowing you to write off 100 percent of your investment in the first year. For example, if you invest $100K, you can immediately reduce your taxable income by the full amount, providing significant and quick tax relief.[79]

This strategy does *not* come with the strict IRS guidelines required for real estate professional status, making it accessible to a broader range of investors, including W2 earners. The ability to deduct the full value of your investment in the first year makes syndicated ATM funds an excellent option for those looking to minimize taxes while benefiting from reliable cash flow.

Despite the rise of digital payments, ATMs remain essential for cash transactions in many major cities, especially for the unbanked and those who have been excluded from traditional banking systems. Lots of people still rely on ATMs to cash checks and this is unlikely to change anytime soon.

Much like the oil funds I mentioned earlier, the IRS does not recapture accelerated depreciation on ATM funds. So you won't need a 1031 exchange to defer taxes, which makes this a simple investment from a tax perspective.

Another advantage of syndicated ATM funds is that many of them return investors' capital in less than two years. Getting your initial investment back quickly reduces your risk. If the deal doesn't perform well in, say, year four, you'll have already recouped your capital, minimising potential losses. Plus, this quick return allows you to reinvest in other opportunities sooner, so you can double the number of investments you're in every two years and accelerate your wealth-generation.

The combination of steady demand, upfront depreciation, quick return of capital, and the absence of depreciation recapture makes syndicated ATM funds a simple, tax-efficient investment.

One of the most effective ways to find quality syndications in any asset class is to meet lots of fund managers at investment conferences. These events are prime opportunities to socialize with industry leaders, gain insider insights, and uncover quality investment opportunities that are not readily available to the general public. By engaging directly with asset managers, you can ask specific questions and gauge the expertise of the individuals behind each syndication. This will allow you to compare syndication strategies, risk profiles, and projected returns so you can make better decisions about where to invest your capital.

That said, I'd like to make your search easier by providing you with resources to streamline your search. For the latest information on the syndications I'm currently investing in, visit **syndication.natehambrick.com** for up-to-date resources and syndication partners.

The Many Faces of the LLC

One of the core strategies to not own anything on paper is to leverage the limited liability company (LLC), a true chameleon in the legal landscape. An LLC combines the robust liability protection of a corporation with the flexible tax benefits of a partnership, making it a powerful tool for business owners.

The LLC is a liability shield. It gives the entrepreneur the freedom to pursue business ventures with the assurance that their personal assets are protected from the debts and obligations of their enterprise. The strategic use of multiple LLCs can be a powerful deterrent to litigation. By compartmentalizing assets across multiple LLCs, entrepreneurs can create a labyrinthine structure that obscures the full scope of their holdings. Each LLC acts as an independent cell, immune to the volatility of the others, ensuring that risk in one venture does not bleed into another. It's not just about creating a facade to deter litigants (although that result will be achieved); it's about the intelligent allocation of assets to minimize risk.[80]

At the same time, the LLC is also a conduit for financial efficiency, particularly through the lens of taxation, allowing profits to flow directly to members without the bite of corporate taxes. This single layer of taxation, a departure from the double taxation seen in corporations, not only simplifies the tax process, but also positions the LLC as an attractive option for those seeking to maximize their after-tax income. The appeal of the LLC extends to those who may benefit from the S corporation designation. Members can draw reasonable salaries, upon which employment taxes are due, and then receive any remaining profits as dividends, which in some cases are taxed at a much lower rate and not subject to self-employment tax. This salary and dividend distribution strategy is akin to a well-choreographed financial ballet, balancing the act of maximum income with minimal tax liability.

Beyond liability and tax advantages, the LLC structure commands respect and credibility in the business world. It signals to potential investors and lenders that the business is a serious entity, grounded in formal structure and intent on longevity. This perception can open doors to capital and foster growth that might otherwise be unattainable for sole proprietorships or informal partnerships.

As you take advantage of the power that the LLC offers you, it's important to remember that these business structures require strict compliance and meticulous record keeping to ensure that your financial records accurately reflect the company's transactions and that any deductions claimed are justified. Tax *avoidance* is the star on your Christmas tree, but tax *evasion* will land you in jail.

Again, having a competent tax planner can be life changing. I don't need to know every leverage point in the tax code; instead, I use Law Nine (Master Your Strengths; Ignore the Rest), and I let someone else structure everything to my advantage. I bring my income streams to my tax advisor, and they tell me where to open LLCs and S corps, and where to park my money.

For those who want to take this a step further, there is also a way to use an LLC to own shares of an S corporation, adding an extra layer of protection so you don't own anything on paper. By holding the S corp shares within an LLC, business owners can further insulate their personal assets from the risks and liabilities associated with their business operations.

Layering Trusts and LLCs

The more successful you are, the more you need to protect what you've built. Unfortunately, not everyone in this world wants what's best for you. There are people whose primary income comes from suing and exploiting legal loopholes to take what you've built. While some of this can be prevented with background checks, it is important to prepare in advance.

LLCs offer protection. Trusts provide anonymity.

Limited liability companies provide a legal structure that protects its owners from personal liability for the debts and obligations of the business. This means that the personal assets of the members are generally protected if the LLC is sued or incurs debt.

Trusts, when properly structured, provide anonymity. The assets held in the trust are legally owned by the trust itself, not by the individual who created the trust (the grantor). This separation can help keep ownership information private and shield the true owner's identity from public records and potential litigants. If your moocher doesn't know who you are or doesn't know what you own, it's hard to sue you.

This section outlines essential steps you can take to make it a little more difficult from someone to sue you. I will include one of the many ways to layer trusts and LLCs for anonymity and protection, but I recommend using a professional to set yours up to maximize the benefits for your situation.

Step one is to establish an irrevocable trust. The irrevocable nature of these trusts ensures that once assets are placed in them, they cannot be changed or revoked, thus protecting them from future claims or creditors.

Step two is to appoint a trustee of your trust who isn't you. Appoint a family member with a different last name, such as a sister, cousin, or married daughter. This person should be someone you trust implicitly but whose name is not directly associated with you. Alternatively, consider using a professional trust service to add an extra layer of anonymity and professionalism.

Your trust documents should contain specific provisions to maximize protection and privacy. The trustee's powers should be limited, preventing him or her from buying, selling, or transferring assets without specific instructions outlined in the trust. Additionally, a confidentiality clause should be included that legally binds the trustee to confidentiality and prevents him or her from disclosing any information about the trust.

Be sure to set up a beneficiary clause by naming the beneficiary as an LLC that you control. This LLC will hold the beneficial interest in the trust assets. You may also want to create multiple LLCs to further diversify risk and avoid cross-liability. Each LLC should hold different assets and be structured with nominee managers or directors to distance your name from the entities. This strategy not only spreads risk but also complicates any legal attempts to seize your assets.

Register the trustee's post office box address in a state known for strong asset protection laws, such as Delaware, Nevada, or Wyoming. Use a reputable mail forwarding service that will scan the mail sent to your out-of-state PO box and email it to you. This will help distance your personal location from the trust.

Transfer ownership of your assets to the respective LLCs, making sure that title to each asset is properly transferred to avoid legal complications. Use quitclaim deeds or warranty deeds for real estate transfers to ensure proper recording with the local county.

This is one of the many ways to layer trusts with LLCs, but I don't recommend setting this up on your own. Your job is to understand that layering trusts and LLCs will protect you. Your attorney's job is to set this up, so hire an experienced attorney who specializes in asset protection and estate planning to structure and draft the necessary trust documents. This will ensure compliance with state and federal laws while maximizing your legal protection.

By combining your trusts and LLCs in this way, you protect yourself in many ways. The litigant has to identify the owner of the trust, which should take them a while since the address is registered out of state. From there, they would have to figure out how much equity is in the corresponding LLC and decide if there's enough capital to make any of this worthwhile. Then they have to buy a plane ticket to fly to an out-of-state PO box to serve papers on someone who doesn't live there. At the end of the day, it's a total mess, and lawyers who make their living suing everyone for anything to see what sticks would much rather drop you so they can focus on easier targets.

It's also important to understand that corporations do not automatically protect you from all liability 100 percent of the time. No matter how well a corporation is formed, in a court of law, all the prosecutor has to do is find a *crack* in the corporate veil to hold you personally liable. This *crack* can be anything from failing to properly maintain corporate records, commingling personal and business finances, or engaging in fraudulent activities. Once a court finds this breach, the legal protections of the corporate entity may be disregarded, and your personal assets may be exposed to satisfy business debts or legal judgments.

So, while they're not completely impenetrable, the primary function of using trusts and LLCs is to make it significantly more difficult for someone to successfully sue you and to deter the majority of frivolous lawsuits.

Remember, the ultimate goal is to own nothing on paper. When combined together, the use of depreciation, LLCs, and trusts, form the foundation for the seventeenth law of leverage: Don't own anything on paper. These tools provide a shield against liability, limit tax obligations, and enhance business credibility.

Reality Check

Do you pay more taxes than a billionaire?

Millions of Americans lose their financial margin in taxation, without leveraging government incentives that allow them to keep more of their hard-earned money.

Even if it takes a while, it's important to slowly increase the gap between what you actually earn and what you earn on paper. Even if you only put $50K into syndicated real estate or oil funds each year, that would reduce your taxable income by $25K to $50K per year. The compounding effect of that over time would be a game changer.

You might even think about buying your next car in your LLC and using "business income" to pay for it pre-tax. But don't take it from me—hire a tax planner to help you move things around; create LLCs and S corps to help you lower your income on paper.

These levers compound on each other. The money you save in taxes, along with the income you generate, can be used to accelerate the other seventeen laws and get you further, faster.

P.S. Don't worry about the taxman. Even though you're saving taxes by using the strategies in this chapter, he'll still get his fair share out of you through sales tax, property tax, licenses, and fees. You're still a good citizen, even if you reduce your tax burden.

Leveraged Action Steps

	Leveraged Action Steps	Your Notes
#1	**Asset Protection:** How can you leverage an LLC to protect your assets?	
#2	**Asset Reallocation:** What assets do you currently have that could be held under a corporate entity instead?	
#3	**Expense Evaluation:** What business expenses are you currently paying for post-tax (cars, cell phone, gas, etc.) that you could be purchasing pre-tax?	
#4	**Income Restructuring:** Where could you restructure your income streams to lower your taxes?	

Chapter Seventeen Takeaway

LAW SEVENTEEN
Leverage corporate entities to limit liability, reduce taxes, and increase privacy.

Harness the Attention Economy

"The attention economy is not growing,
which means we have to grab the attention
that someone else has today."

—Brent Leary (co-founder of CRM Essentials, advisor, and author)

Throughout human history, the pursuit of valuable resources has been at the forefront of social evolution.

In ancient times, we were captivated by the spice trade, a pursuit that drove explorers across uncharted seas and led to the discovery of new lands. Spices such as pepper, cinnamon, and cloves were highly coveted, often worth their weight in gold. This quest not only fueled economic growth but also facilitated cultural exchange and shaped global trade routes.

The twentieth century witnessed the oil boom, where black gold became the lifeblood of modern economies. Oil-powered industries fueled transportation and transformed geopolitical landscapes. Nations and corporations that controlled oil reserves wielded immense power, and the quest for this resource sparked conflicts and alliances that continue to influence global politics today.

Limited, valuable resources have driven industries, fueled economies, and shaped geopolitical landscapes throughout our history. But now, as we move deeper into the twenty-first century, a new kind of resource has emerged as the cornerstone of economic power. It's not one mined from the depths of the earth but one that resides in our collective consciousness: attention.

If traditional resources such as oil and minerals were the engines of the industrial age, attention is the currency of the information age. In this new economy, *mining* for attention does not require drills and excavators. Instead, it requires content and connectivity. The platforms that capture attention have become the new oil fields, and the companies that control these platforms wield power comparable to the oil magnates of the past.

The attention economy operates on the principle that human attention is finite, making it a highly coveted resource. The platforms that host people's attention are the doorways through which businesses must pass to reach their audience—it's the first step on the path to engagement, conversion, and profit.

The digital marketplace is where that attention is quantified and monetized. Clicks, views, and time spent with content have become the lifeblood of modern businesses. Today's engagement translates into tomorrow's leads, customers, and revenue. The winners in this new economy are those who understand that attention is finite and know how to stand out in the endless sea of distractions.

Monetizing attention is an art form—it requires creating content that not only catches the eye but inspires the viewer to take an action that leads to profit. The key is to craft a narrative or offer that resonates so deeply with the audience that it compels them to invest their time and, ultimately, their money.

In the pantheon of those who have mastered this art is the Kardashian-Jenner family. They have turned the drama business into a lucrative empire. Their approach is a masterclass in attention economics—every story, every post, every product launch, every endorsement is tailored to capture and hold the public's interest. They successfully create a cycle of attention that continually feeds their various business ventures.

For any business today, celebrity-driven or not, capturing attention is the first nonnegotiable step toward growth. For retail, this could mean creating visually stunning displays; for tech companies, it might involve producing educational content on new technology; and for entertainment, it could be compelling storytelling or the latest gossip. It's only once you have attention that you can begin to turn it into long-term engagement.

This evolution from physical resources to cognitive engagement reflects the ongoing adaptability and innovation of human societies, demonstrating that while the tools and mediums may change, the fundamental drive for influence and prosperity remains constant.

Those who can navigate these technological advances while staying attuned to shifts in consumer behavior will find themselves at the forefront of this attention economy.

Case Studies

When it comes to whiskey and tequila, most of us are familiar with Jameson and Jose Cuervo. These brands have rich histories dating back more than two centuries, to 1780 and 1758, respectively.[81] Their legacies include acquiring farmland, building distilleries, receiving royal patronage, surviving wars, enduring boycotts and prohibitions, and surviving multiple takeover attempts, all while maintaining multigenerational family leadership.

However, new brands like Proper No. Twelve whiskey and Teremana Tequila are rapidly gaining popularity. Proper No. Twelve, launched by Irish boxer Conor McGregor, already has twice as many Instagram followers as Jameson.[82] Teremana Tequila, endorsed by Dwayne "The Rock" Johnson, has become one of the fastest-growing tequila brands in history.[83]

How are these relatively new brands challenging these legendary labels?

Enter the influencer.

As previously mentioned, Conor McGregor promotes Proper No. Twelve and Teremana Tequila is endorsed by Dwayne "The Rock" Johnson, who owns a 30 percent stake in the $3.5 billion brand.[84]

These aren't your typical mom-and-pop business owners; they are influencers with millions of loyal followers who leverage their personal brands to fuel their businesses. Proper No. Twelve didn't rely on traditional TV or radio ads, yet it sold an impressive 6 million bottles in just two and a half years, thanks to Conor McGregor's hands-on promotion and his passionate fan base.[85] Similarly, Teremana Tequila sells more than one million nine-liter cases annually, driven by The Rock's vast global following and his genuine engagement with consumers.[86]

Yesterday's greatest sources of wealth were derived from *oil*. The largest organizations of the last century, such as Aramco, Chevron, and Exxon Mobil, were built on oil, gas, energy, and power.

Today, however, four of the five largest organizations in the world—Apple, Microsoft, Amazon, and Alphabet (Google)—are built on *attention*. The old wealth came from underneath the ground; new wealth comes from capturing attention.[87]

Content + Attention = Wealth

In July 2022, *Variety* magazine did a feature on Jimmy Donaldson, better known on YouTube as MrBeast. MrBeast's channel has just passed 100 million subscribers. In his channel, he is quite expressive about his ambitious net worth goal of *$100 billion*.

The reason critics haven't laughed at this massive number is because attention is increasingly becoming the most valuable resource, and MrBeast has loads of it.

Simply put, we all have only so much attention to give to brands. Our attention is both scarce and precious.

And it's getting harder and harder to get a piece of that attention.

Those who have that attention—and can *keep it*—will also have the leverage to create massive wealth.

Let's go back to Conor McGregor and Dwayne Johnson and their respective alcohol brands for a moment. There are two *big* things that both fighter influencers got right with their brands that many influencers, attention-seekers, and content-monetizers don't.

1. Timing: Conor and Dwayne have been building their personal brands for a long time. (In The Rock's case, it's been over twenty years.) For decades, they amassed an audience that loved and respected them and didn't try to sell them anything. As Apple's former chief evangelist Guy Kawasaki explains, "When you enchant people, your goal is not to make money from them or to get them to do what you want, but to fill them with great delight." That's what both fighters did for decades.

2. Alignment: Both products that were eventually launched were perfectly aligned with what these men embodied and what their audiences admired them for. It's also important to note that The Rock has successfully cultivated several distinct audiences—the family-friendly actor who caters to children with movies like *The Game Plan* and *Moana*, and the total badass fitness junkie who sells Under Armour and Teremana Tequila.

Simply put, you need to tailor your products to the desires of your audience and deliver exponentially more value to them than you receive in return. This is where scale comes into play. By creating content that can be consumed by the masses, you can focus your efforts on producing a limited number of high-quality pieces—say, a few hundred videos—that reach millions of people. If those people consume your content for years and eventually buy your products, you've successfully provided them with far more value than the money they spent with you.

Practical Steps for Brand Building

Tapping into the attention economy starts with a simple principle: provide simple solutions to people's real challenges. Ask yourself, "What tangible value will my audience get in exchange for their attention?" Your ability to succinctly answer this question will be the foundation for creating compelling content people actually need.

Position yourself as an expert in your field—then commit to becoming more of an expert every day. Knowledge compounds on itself, so you'll learn more as you share what you currently know. Once you have a clear message that resonates with somebody, spread it widely and consistently to everybody. Persistence is key. Keep refining your message until it clicks with your audience—whether that takes weeks or years—because once it does, the impact will be life changing.

For those who are hesitant to put themselves out there, let's clear up a common misconception: not everyone needs to be a flashy Instagram influencer to succeed in the attention economy. You don't have to monetize your appearance or manufacture drama like the Kardashians to build a powerful brand. You have the power to define your audience and shape your message according to the goals you've established for yourself.

The audience you choose to serve with your content will have a significant impact on your trajectory. Although the way movie stars and singers monetize attention attracts paparazzi and a whole lot of drama, you can choose to attract attention in a way that doesn't bring all the chaos along with it.

Instead, focus on providing real solutions to people's problems. What if you taught someone something valuable—something that solves their immediate problems, *for free*—and then used that as a lead generation tool to sell paid solutions for their more complex challenges? Even if the problems you're solving are super niche, this can dramatically increase your income. I know this to be true because my income tripled within a year of publishing Crush Your Kryptonite. I just wish I had done it sooner.

I want to simplify the process and give you three ways you can harness the attention economy.

Harness Attention Through Publishing

Mining attention is one of the most profitable laws of leverage because it has infinite scale. I strongly encourage entrepreneurs and sales reps to publish books to mine for the attention they need to grow their businesses. Publishing is more than just a medium for sharing knowledge; it's a cornerstone for establishing your brand in the marketplace. If you own a business and publish a book, you set yourself apart from every other ordinary business owner—you're now an author, which carries a prestigious connotation that can significantly enhance your brand. If you're a sales representative working for a giant corporation and publish a book to generate leads for your employer, you will set yourself apart from every other ordinary sales person. Not only will you have more high quality leads, but your close rate should go up dramatically because people will know you're an expert and because they can verify you online in a grander fashion. I can't tell you how many deals I've pulled across the line because prospects google me and realize I'm not their average rep.

A book also offers a unique blend of authenticity and authority that sets you apart in a crowded field. It allows you to tell your brand's story in your own voice, share your insights, and articulate your business philosophy in a way that cuts through the noise and reaches the highest quality audience. Because there is a lot more intention behind books, the content you create tends to be curated at a higher level, which builds loyalty and trust. Even prospects who don't read your books are more likely to do business with you, just because you wrote one.

Best of all, it's a more subtle way to get attention—no Instagram filter needed.

Brendon Burchard, author of *The Millionaire Messenger*, is a great example of monetizing attention through books. Burchard uses his books as lead magnets to build his coaching and personal development businesses.

His books are his low-ticket offers that introduce readers to his methods and philosophies, which leads them to explore his higher-ticket courses, seminars, and coaching programs.

Here's how Burchard's profit cycle works:

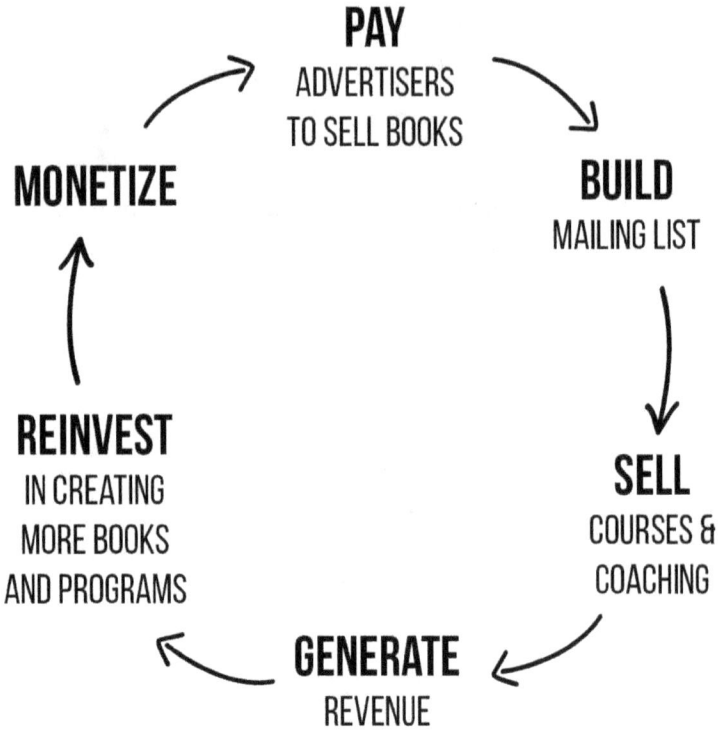

PAY
ADVERTISERS
TO SELL BOOKS

BUILD
MAILING LIST

SELL
COURSES &
COACHING

GENERATE
REVENUE

REINVEST
IN CREATING
MORE BOOKS
AND PROGRAMS

MONETIZE

This model is highly effective because it leverages the book to create a continuous stream of leads and revenue. Leads generated through book funnels are more cost-effective than other lead sources. Content marketing, including book funnels, generates leads at 62 percent less cost than traditional marketing, and the purchases from these leads are 47 percent larger on average than non-nurtured leads.[88, 89] You can adapt a similar approach to leverage publishing a book for high-quality leads for your own business.

Authorship is one of the greatest ways to establish authority and expertise in any field. It is a weight of credibility that few other forms of communication can match. When you publish, you are declaring your depth of knowledge and your unique perspective to the world. This declaration acts as a powerful signal to peers, competitors, and potential customers that you are a serious, knowledgeable professional committed to your area of expertise.

Look at Tim Ferriss, whose book *The 4-Hour Workweek* turned him into a sought-after speaker and podcast host. His book opened opportunities to speak at major business and tech conferences, and eventually, he leveraged his growing reputation to launch his own podcast, which further solidified his status as an authority on personal and professional development.

Brené Brown used her books, like *Daring Greatly*, to share her expertise in social work and psychology, leveraging this to establish herself as a leading figure in discussions on vulnerability and courage. Her books helped her transition from academia to becoming a public figure, with appearances in TED Talks and Netflix specials, further expanding her influence and reinforcing her authority.

I am by no means on their level, but *Crush Your Kryptonite* generated $280K of backend revenue in the first twelve months and gave me more forms of leverage than anything else I've ever done. It's digital real estate that will pay me for decades to come. It generates business consulting clients every single month. The credibility it gives me increases my close rate and gets me on stages at business conferences. It also connects me with other high-profile authors I want to partner with. All of these forms of leverage have made the biggest difference in my life, not to mention in the lives of the people I get to help.

That's why I wrote this book. I wrote it to further expand my leverage and impact, and to help you do the same.

If you want to write and publish a book that generates six figures or more for your business in its first twelve months, go to **natehambrick. com** for free publishing resources.

Harness Attention on YouTube

A second way to harness the attention economy is through YouTube. Marie Forleo, creator of the YouTube channel MarieTV, has used her YouTube channel as a foundational tool to build a highly successful coaching and online education business. She strategically uses video content to generate leads for her business.

Forleo's YouTube channel introduces viewers to her coaching methods and ideologies and encourages them to explore her other offerings, such as online courses and books. The channel serves as a gateway to Forleo's broader educational resources, keeping viewers engaged and continuously purchasing her services.

Here's how Forleo's revenue cycle works:

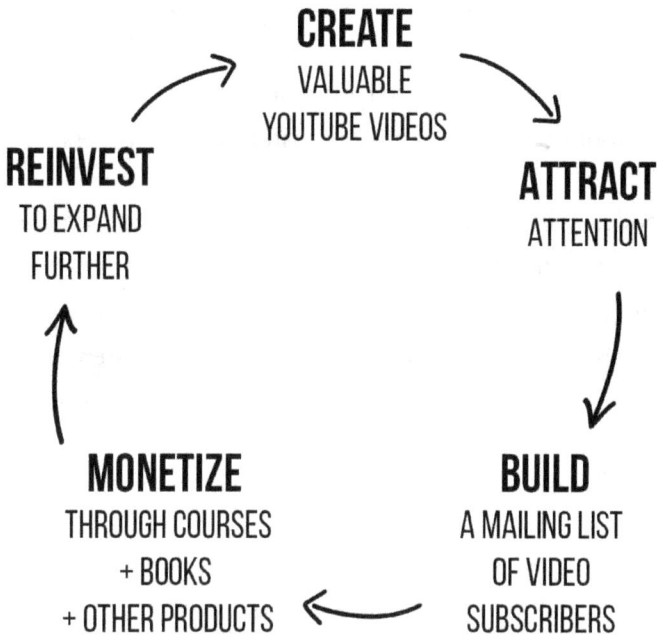

CREATE
VALUABLE
YOUTUBE VIDEOS

ATTRACT
ATTENTION

REINVEST
TO EXPAND
FURTHER

MONETIZE
THROUGH COURSES
+ BOOKS
+ OTHER PRODUCTS

BUILD
A MAILING LIST
OF VIDEO
SUBSCRIBERS

This model is highly effective because it uses YouTube videos to create a continuous stream of leads and revenue. You can adapt a similar approach to leverage your YouTube channel and generate quality leads for your own business.

According to HubSpot, 54 percent of consumers want to see more video content from brands they support.[90] Video content provides a platform for establishing expertise and fostering a deeper connection with your audience, increasing the likelihood of successful conversions that set the stage for sustainable and profitable businesses.

Harness Attention Through Podcasting

Another effective way to harness the attention economy is through podcasting. Take the example of Pat Flynn, host of the *Smart Passive Income* podcast. Flynn has used his podcast as a fundamental lead generation tool to build a highly successful online business.

Flynn's podcast introduces listeners to his business strategies and systems which leads them to explore his other offerings, such as online courses, books, and membership sites. The podcast is an entry point to Flynn's broader educational resources, keeping listeners engaged and invested in his teachings long after they have finished listening.

Here's how Flynn's revenue cycle works:

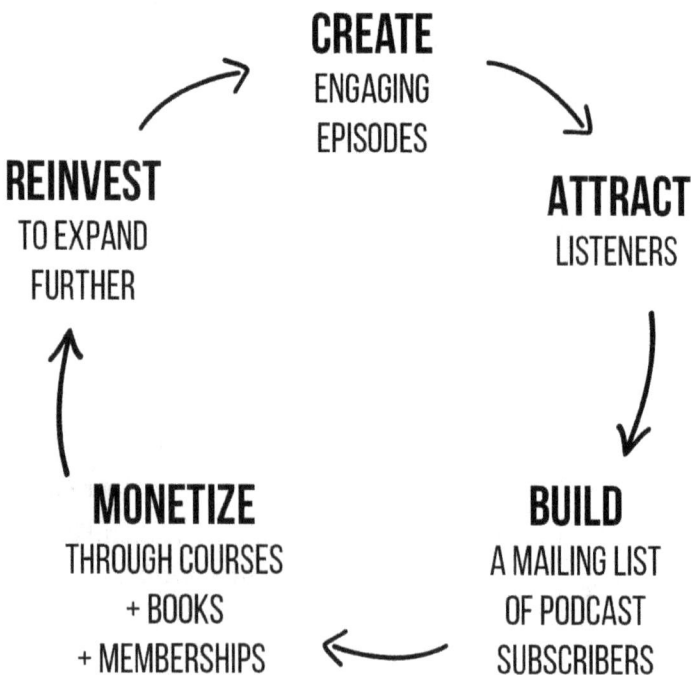

CREATE
ENGAGING
EPISODES

ATTRACT
LISTENERS

REINVEST
TO EXPAND
FURTHER

MONETIZE
THROUGH COURSES
+ BOOKS
+ MEMBERSHIPS

BUILD
A MAILING LIST
OF PODCAST
SUBSCRIBERS

This model is highly effective because podcasts create a continuous stream of leads for his business. You can adapt a similar approach to use your podcast to generate quality leads for your own business.

Podcasting taps into a rich vein of engaged prospects, providing them with valuable content that prepares them for further offers. Data from Edison Research shows that 80 percent of podcast listeners are highly engaged, listening to most (if not all) of every episode they start.[91] This high level of initial engagement translates into more effective leads; and more leads means more business. The trust established with the podcast also improves conversion rates for prospects who heard about the business from other sources, especially for nervous buyers who thoroughly vet businesses online before purchasing. People trust businesses more when they have hundreds of backlinks on Google. This shortens the path to profit and gives the operators more time and resources to grow further.

These are just a few of the many ways to *harness the attention economy*. Identify the platforms and methods that resonate most with you, and leverage them to increase your speed and output of services.

Reality Check

Does your target audience know who you are?

What percent of your market knows you exist? Do the people who need your services think of you when they need help, or is someone else better at grasping their attention?

No matter where you are at exposure-wise, it's always a great time to increase your visibility and reach more people.

If you're great at something, it's important that you share that skill set with the world. It's not just about increasing your monetary gain; it's about increasing your leverage to make the world better.

Remember, attention is a critical component of scale, so increase your online visibility to make the most out of all the other laws of leverage.

Just begin—and keep at it.

Leveraged Action Steps

	Leveraged Action Steps	Your Notes
#1	**Platform Identification:** What platforms (YouTube, Instagram, Amazon, podcasts, etc.) will you focus on to get attention?	
#2	**Content Creation:** List three ideas for content you can create in less than three hours to get someone's attention.	
#3	**Building Authority:** How can you position yourself as an authority in your market?	
#4	**Monetization:** How will you monetize that attention? (Focus on selling products or services you already have.)	

Chapter Eighteen Takeaway

LAW EIGHTEEN

Increase your exposure and visibility to create more opportunities for wealth.

Conclusion

"Impatience with actions, patience with results."

—Naval Ravikant

Each of us has the potential to achieve extraordinary things, but this potential will not be realized through sheer force or tireless effort. Instead, it must be realized through the masterful application of leverage.

As Archimedes famously said, "Give me a lever long enough and a fulcrum on which to place it, and I shall move the world." This ancient wisdom captures the essence of this book and the power that leverage can bring to your life.

Throughout this journey, we've explored the eighteen laws of leverage, each a tool designed to amplify your efforts and multiply your results. Like gears in a well-engineered machine, each act of leverage may seem small and unremarkable on its own, barely noticeable in the daily grind. But as you carefully assemble and align these gears, their cumulative effect becomes a powerful engine of progress, driving you forward faster than you ever thought possible.

The first step in harnessing this power is to recognize the value of those who have come before you and to build on their achievements.

In Law One: *Stand on the Shoulders of Giants*, we learned how to leverage the knowledge and success of others to succeed faster.

In Law Two: *Use Other People's Money (OPM)*, we explored how to leverage capital effectively.

In Law Three: *Use Other People's Time (OPT)*, we recognized that time is our most valuable resource and discussed the importance of delegating the majority of our tasks to others.

In Law Four, *Charge for the Result; Hire by the Hour*, we learned how to charge for the result, outsource by the hour, and pocket the difference.

In Law Five, *Charge for Your Brand to Build Your Brand*, we outlined practical steps for monetizing the brands we currently have to fuel their growth.

In Law Six: *Buy the Victory*, we emphasized that paying for guaranteed results when possible is easier than working for them.

In Law Seven: *Focus on the Profits*, we highlighted the importance of prioritizing profits and paying ourselves first.

In Law Eight: *Think More Than You Work*, we talked about how our strategy will take us further than relentless hard work.

In Law Nine: *Master Your Strengths; Ignore the Rest*, we learned to focus the majority of our effort on developing our highest leverage skills to maximize the results we get from our work.

In Law Ten: *Conserve Your Power*, we discussed the need to de-prioritize low-leverage tasks to maximize output and reduce burnout.

In Law Eleven: *Swim With the Tide*, we learned to take advantage of economic trends and opportunities instead of fighting them.

In Law Twelve: *Ride the Coattails of Success*, we talked about how to align ourselves with successful individuals to benefit from their network and success.

In Law Thirteen: *Buy Assets; Limit Liabilities*, we found ways to make life easier by allowing our assets to do the heavy lifting for us.

In Law Fourteen: *Create Once; Sell Forever*, we talked about how to create scalable products that can be sold infinitely.

In Law Fifteen: *Don't Do Things You Hate*, we focused on finding work that allows us to thrive, in areas we can dominate.

In Law Sixteen: *Don't Work for Money*, we worked on positioning ourselves so money follows us instead of chasing a paycheck.

In Law Seventeen: *Don't Own Anything on Paper*, we explored ways to leverage corporate entities to limit liability, lower taxes, and keep wealth private.

And in Law Eighteen: *Harness the Attention Economy*, we discussed the importance of increasing our exposure and visibility to create more opportunity.

The beauty of leverage is that it's accessible to everyone. It does not discriminate by birth, wealth, or status; it is available to all who recognize its potential and choose to use it. By understanding the strategic points where effort yields the highest return, you can optimize your actions to create maximum impact with minimal energy. This is the heart of leverage—the intelligent amplification of your efforts that leads to exponential wealth and success.

In closing, remember that the journey of leveraging is continuous and ever-evolving. As the world around us changes, the points of leverage shift, and new opportunities surface. Stay vigilant and adaptable, always ready to apply the laws you have learned in innovative ways. Cultivate the leverage mindset: Seek efficiency, think strategically, and act boldly.

Let *The 18 Laws of Leverage* be your guide to transcending the ordinary limits of effort and achieving the extraordinary. As you close this book, think of it not as the end of your learning but as the foundation of a lifelong practice. The principles in these pages are not just theories, but practical tools that, when applied with skill and foresight, have the power to move mountains for you.

With a little luck and a lot of leverage, there is no limit to what you can accomplish.

Notes

1. Ramish Cheema, "5 Biggest Employers in the World," Insider Money Blog, https://www.insidermonkey.com/blog/5-biggest-employers-in-the-world-1102540/5/.

2. Sam DeHority, "Expert Tips from Business Success and NBA Owner Mark Cuban," MensJournal.com, https://www.mensjournal.com/sports/mark-cuban-sport-business/.

3. Taylor Locke, "This is Mark Cuban's 'most underrated' skill as a businessman, according to his former professor," CNBC, https://www.cnbc.com/2021/02/09/mark-cubans-underrated-skill-as-businessman.html.

4. Rick Warren, "Disciples of Jesus Never Stop Learning," PastorRick.com, https://pastorrick.com/devotional/english/full-post/disciples-of-jesus-never-stop-learning/.

5. Mike Myatt, "What All Great Leaders Have In Common," N2Growth Blog, https://www.n2growth.com/the-learning-ceo/.

6. Kevan Lee, "Warren Buffett's Best Kept Secret to Success: The Art of Reading, Remembering, and Retaining More Books," Buffer.com, https://buffer.com/resources/how-to-read-more-and-remember-it-all/.

7. Eric Jorgenson, "Learn to love to read," The Almanack of Naval Ravikant, https://www.navalmanack.com/almanack-of-naval-ravikant/learn-to-love-to-read.

8. Rob Errera, "Eye-Popping Book and Reading Statistics [2023]," https://www.tonerbuzz.com/blog/book-and-reading-statistics/.

9. Laura Beck, "Robert Kiyosaki Says These Are the 2 Real Estate Investing Rules That Keep Him Rich – and the 5 Markets He Avoids 'Like a Plague.'" Yahoo Finance, https://finance.yahoo.com/news/robert-kiyosaki-says-2-real-160050476.html.

10. CPI Inflation Calculator, In2013dollars.com, "$100 in 1920 Is Worth $1,576.51 Today," https://www.in2013dollars.com/us/inflation/1920?amount=100.

11. Alex Hormozi, "Get RICH in 2023: Live like you're broke," https://www.youtube.com/watch?v=Day0yToqeco&t=753s&ab_channel=AlexHormozi.

12. Eric Levenson, "Bestselling Spy Author Tom Clancy Has Died," *The Atlantic*, https://www.theatlantic.com/national/archive/2013/10/tom-clancy-has-died-spy-author/310404/.

13. Bradley J. Birzer, "Who Wrote Tom Clancy's Last Novels?" The Imaginative Conservative Blog, https://theimaginativeconservative.org/2016/02/who-wrote-tom-clancys-last-novels.html#:~:text=Teeth%20of%20the%20Tiger%20is,%2C%20most%20often%2C%20Mark%20Greaney.

14. Kiran Rathee, "Pegatron follows Foxconn to make iPhone 14 in India," https://telecom.economictimes.indiatimes.com/news/pegatron-follows-foxconn-to-make-iphone-14-in-india/95311448.

15. Travis Shaw, "France and the American Revolution," American Battlefield Trust, www.battlefields.org/learn/articles/france-american-revolution.

16. Zoe Chace, (2011, June 30), "How much does it cost to make a hit song?" *NPR*, https://www.npr.org/sections/money/2011/07/05/137530847/how-much-does-it-cost-to-make-a-hit-song.

17. Stacy Wells, "Top Paid Influencers and Brand Ambassadors," GetRoster, www.getroster.com/blog/top-paid-influencers-and-brand-ambassadors/.

18. Nick Hall, "15 Highest Paid Celebrities on Instagram," Man of Many, www.manofmany.com/lifestyle/highest-paid-celebrities-instagram.

19. Wikipedia, "Ariana Grande," https://en.wikipedia.org/wiki/Ariana_Grande.

20. Madeline Berg, "Fenty's Fortune: Rihanna Is Now Officially A Billionaire," *Forbes*, https://www.forbes.com/sites/maddieberg/2021/08/04/fentys-fortune-rihanna-is-now-officially-a-billionaire/?sh=36b2467f7c96.

21. Dakotah Blanton, "15 Richest Female Singers In The World," Music Grotto, https://www.musicgrotto.com/richest-female-singers-in-the-world/.

22. Roland Martin, "Carnegie Steel Company," Britannica, https://www.britannica.com/topic/Carnegie-Steel-Company.

23. Microsoft. "Acquisition History," Microsoft Investor Relations, https://www.microsoft.com/en-us/Investor/acquisition-history.aspx.

24. Neil Patel, "90% Of Startups Fail: Here's What You Need To Know About The 10%," Forbes, https://www.forbes.com/sites/neilpatel/2015/01/16/90-of-startups-will-fail-heres-what-you-need-to-know-about-the-10/?sh=60c4ae496679.

25. Bureau of Labor Statistics, "Occupational employment and wages – May 2020," US. Department of Labor, https://www.bls.gov/news.release/archives/ocwage_03312021.pdf.

26. Payscale, "Blockchain Engineer Salary," https://www.payscale.com/research/US/Job.

27. Dan Blystone, "The History of Uber," Investopedia, www.investopedia.com/articles/personal-finance/111015/story-uber.asp.

28. Sean Blanda, "The Jeff Bezos School of Long-Term Thinking," Sean Blanda, www.seanblanda.com/the-jeff-bezos-school-of-long-term-thinking/.

29. Mental Health America, "Mind the Workplace: MHA Workplace Health Survey 2021," Mental Health America, https://www.mhanational.

org/sites/default/files/Mind%20the%20Workplace%20-%20MHA%20
Workplace%20Health%20Survey%202021%202.12.21.pdf.

30. The American Institute of Stress, "Workplace Stress," https://www.stress.org/workplace-stress.

31. Worldometer, "GDP by Country," https://www.worldometers.info/gdp/gdp-by-country/.

32. Fiveable, "Google's 20 Percent Time," https://library.fiveable.me/key-terms/innovation-management/googles-20percent-time.

33. Chatra, "Zappos and the Path to Customer Happiness," https://chatra.com/books/customer-service-excellence-examples/02-zappos-and-the-path-to-customer-happiness/.

34. Paul Raeburn, "Arianna Huffington: Collapse from exhaustion was wake-up call," Today.com, https://www.today.com/health/arianna-huffington-collapse-exhaustion-was-wake-call-2d79644042.

35. Arianna Huffington, "10 Years Ago I Collapsed From Burnout and Exhaustion, And It's The Best Thing That Could Have Happened To Me," Medium.com, https://medium.com/thrive-global/10-years-ago-i-collapsed-from-burnout-and-exhaustion-and-its-the-best-thing-that-could-have-b1409f16585d.

36. World Health Organization, "Burn-out an 'occupational phenomenon': International Classification of Diseases," News, World Health Organization, https://www.who.int/news/item/28-05-2019-burn-out-an-occupational-phenomenon-international-classification-of-diseases.

37. Jen Fisher, "Workplace Burnout Survey - Burnout without borders," Deloitte, https://www2.deloitte.com/us/en/pages/about-deloitte/articles/burnout-survey.html.

38. Patrick Kariuki, "How and When Did Netflix Start? A Brief History of the Company," MakeUseOf Blog, https://www.makeuseof.com/how-when-netflix-start-brief-company-history/.

39. Larissa Zageris, "What Happened to Blockbuster Video & Why It Closed." Money Digest, https://www.moneydigest.com/1687970/what-happened-to-blockbuster-video-why-it-closed/.

40. Kurt Schlosser, "'Developers, developers, developers!' Ballmer and Sinofsky talk Microsoft, memes, more in Clubhouse," Geekwire, https://www.geekwire.com/2021/developers-developers-developers-ballmer-sinofsky-talk-microsoft-memes-clubhouse/.

41. Bloomberg, "Bloomberg Billionaires Index" Bloomberg. com, https://www.bloomberg.com/billionaires/.

42. Encyclopaedia Britannica Inc., "Vera Wang," https://www.britannica.com/biography/Vera-Wang.

43. "Explained: Money Matters—How Nykaa's Falguni Nayar Has Become India's Richest Self-Made Woman." *Firstpost*, https://www.firstpost.com/explainers/explained-money-matters-how-nykaas-falguni-nayar-has-become-indias-richest-self-made-woman-11304721.html.

54. Pierre Azoulay, Benjamin F. Jones, J. Daniel Kim, and Javier Miranda, "Research: The Average Age of a Successful Startup Founder Is 45," Harvard Business Review, https://hbr.org/2018/07/research-the-average-age-of-a-successful-startup-founder-is-45.

44. GEM Consortium, "Global Entrepreneurship Monitor 2022/2023 United States Report," https://www.gemconsortium.org/report/global-entrepreneurship-monitor-2022-2023-united-states-report.

45. Oliver Lewis, "Generation Z Is More Entrepreneurial and Willing to Take Financial Risks, Survey Finds," The Sun, www.thesun.co.uk/money/30329546/generation-z-entrepreneurial-financial-risk.

46. Pierre Azoulay, Benjamin F. Jones, J. Daniel Kim, and Javier Miranda, "Research: The Average Age of a Successful Startup Founder Is 45," Harvard Business Review, https://hbr.org/2018/07/research-the-average-age-of-a-successful-startup-founder-is-45.

47. Jessica Dickler, "62% of Americans are still living paycheck to paycheck, making it 'the main financial lifestyle,' report finds,"

CNBC, https://www.cnbc.com/2023/10/31/62percent-of-americans-still-live-paycheck-to-paycheck-amid-inflation.html.

48. WallStreetZen, "Pfizer Statistics - Pfizer Facts, Stats, Trends & Data (2024)," https://www.wallstreetzen.com/stocks/us/nyse/pfe/statistics.

49. Starbucks Investor Relations, "Starbucks Reports Q4 and Full Year Fiscal 2023 Results," https://investor.starbucks.com/news/financial-releases/news-details/2023/Starbucks-Reports-Q4-and-Full-Year-Fiscal-2023-Results/default.aspx.

50. Ash Turner, "How Many iPhones Have Been Sold?" https://www.bankmycell.com/blog/how-many-iphones-have-been-sold/.

51. Statista, "Revenue of Salesforce.com Broken Down by Cloud Service 2015-2024," https://www.statista.com/statistics/513638/total-revenue-of-salesforce-by-cloud-service/.

52. Liz Hurley, "MasterClass Statistics (2023)," https://learnopoly.com/masterclass-statistics/.

53. Jason Wise, "How Many Employees Does WhatsApp Have in 2023?" *EarthWeb*, 2023, https://earthweb.com/blog/whatsapp-employees/.

54. Ryan Weeks, "Bored Ape Yacht Club Crosses $1 Billion in Total Sales," *The Block*, https://www.theblock.co/linked/129084/bored-ape-yacht-club-crosses-1-billion-in-total-sales.

55. Stephen King, *On Writing*, Simon & Schuster, https://books.google.co.in/books/about/On_Writing.html?id=d999Z2KbZJYC&redir_esc=y.

56. Heather Taylor, "Top 10 Richest Authors in the World," Yahoo Finance, https://finance.yahoo.com/news/top-10-richest-authors-world-110026363.html#:~:text=Stephen%20King&text=King%27s%20net%20worth%20is%20%24500,%22%20and%20%22Salem%27s%20Lot.%22.

57. Alex Crippen, "Warren Buffett Shares His Secret: How You Can 'Tap Dance to Work,'" CNBC, https://www.cnbc.com/2012/11/21/warren-buffett-shares-his-secret-how-you-can-tap-dance-to-work.html.

58. Andy Edwards, "Lionel Messi, Sergio Busquets unveiled by Inter Miami," NBC Sports, https://www.nbcsports.com/soccer/news/lionel-messi-chooses-inter-miami-over-saudi-arabia-mega-offer.

59. Justin Harper, "LeBron James Increases Stake in Liverpool Football Club," *BBC News*, https://www.bbc.com/news/business-56424551.

60. Derek Saul, "Tesla Stock Hits 4-Month High As Elon Musk's Net Worth Soars," *Forbes*, https://www.forbes.com/sites/dereksaul/2023/06/02/tesla-stock-hits-4-month-high-as-elon-musks-net-worth-soars/?sh=5002381b6b91#:~:text=Surprising%20Fact,peak%20of%20about%20%20%24320%20billion.

61. AndSimple, "Elon Musk's Family Office and Excession LLC," https://andsimple.co/cases/elon-musks-family-office-and-excession-llc/.

62. Julia Kagan, "What Is an S Corp?" Investopedia, https://www.investopedia.com/terms/s/subchapters.asp.

63. Grant Cardone, Instagram, https://www.instagram.com/p/Crd0zdzIQ-t/.

64. Sarah Hansen, "Richest Americans—Including Bezos, Musk And Buffett—Paid Federal Income Taxes Equaling Just 3.4% Of $401 Billion In New Wealth, Bombshell Report Shows," *Forbes*, https://www.forbes.com/sites/sarahhansen/2021/06/08/richest-americans-including-bezos-musk-and-buffett-paid-federal-income-taxes-equaling-just-34-of-401-billion-in-new-wealth-bombshell-report-shows/?sh=2479d7cd7fe1.

65. Julia Kagan, "Tax Expense: Definition, Calculation, and Effect on Earnings," Investopedia, www.investopedia.com/terms/t/tax-expense.asp.

66. Jeff Macke, "Coke stock pop nets Warren Buffett $500 million," Yahoo, https://finance.yahoo.com/news/coke-stock-pop-nets-warren-buffett--500-million-174448096.html.

67. Katie Lobosco, "Coke CEO's skips bonus, still gets big raise," CNN Business, https://money.cnn.com/2015/03/12/news/companies/coca-cola-ceo-pay/index.html.

68. Maurie Backman, "Why Does Billionaire Warren Buffett Pay a Lower Tax Rate Than His Secretary?" The Motley Fool, https://www.fool.com/taxes/2020/09/25/why-does-billionaire-warren-buffett-pay-a-lower-ta/#:~:text=So%20why%20is%20it%20that,lower%20rate%20than%20ordinary%20income.

69. Jason Watson, "Three different types of income - Know the tax rates," WCG Inc. https://wcginc.com/kb/three-types-of-income/.

70. ProPublica, "Eight Takeaways From ProPublica's Investigation of How Sports Owners Use Their Teams to Avoid Taxes," ProPublica, https://www.propublica.org/article/eight-takeaways-from-propublicas-investigation-of-how-sports-owners-use-their-teams-to-avoid-taxes.

71. Jason Thompson, "Cost Segregation FAQs," Moss Adams, www.mossadams.com/articles/2021/08/cost-segregation-faqs.

72. Internal Revenue Service, "Tax Cuts and Jobs Act: A Comparison for Businesses," https://www.irs.gov/newsroom/tax-cuts-and-jobs-act-a-comparison-for-businesses.

73. Daniel Goodwin, "1031 Exchange Rules You Need to Know," Kiplinger, www.kiplinger.com/real-estate/1031-exchange-rules-you-need-to-know.

74. George F. Bearup, J.D., "Stepped-Up Basis: A Short History and Why It's Back in the News," Greenleaf Trust, https://greenleaftrust.com/missives/stepped-up-basis-a-short-history-and-why-its-back-in-the-news/.

75. U.S. Securities and Exchange Commission, "Accredited Investors," SEC.gov, U.S. Securities and Exchange Commission, https://www.sec.gov/resources-small-businesses/capital-raising-building-blocks/accredited-investors.

76. Tony Nitti, CPA, MST, "Navigating the Real Estate Professional Rules," The Tax Adviser, American Institute of CPAs, https://www.thetaxadviser.com/issues/2017/mar/navigating-real-estate-professional-rules.html.

77. Jeremy Sompels and Jonathan Winterkorn, "The TCJA 100 Percent Bonus Depreciation Starts to Phase out after 2022," Plante Moran, https://www.plantemoran.com/explore-our-thinking/insight/2022/08/the-tcja-100-percent-bonus-depreciation-starts-to-phase-out-after-2022.

78. Mike Dowd, "Intangible Drilling Costs | IDC Tax Considerations | Denver CPA Firm." Hanson & Co., https://www.hanson-cpa.com/intangible-drilling-costs/.

79. Bronson Hill, "The Secret of How ATM Machine Investing Works," Bronson Equity, https://bronsonequity.com/the-secret-of-how-atm-machine-investing-works/.

80. James S. Bailey, "Should You Form More Than One LLC for Your Business?" Bailey & Peterson PC, https://www.b-p-law.com/news-events--resources/should-you-form-more-than-one-llc-for-your-business.

81. Tom Bruce-Gardyne, "Jose Cuervo: a brand history," The Spirits Business Blog, https://www.thespiritsbusiness.com/2019/06/jose-cuervo-a-brand-history/.

82. Donagh Corby, "Social media expert reveals why Conor McGregor's new Proper 12 whiskey can surpass Jameson," Irish Mirror, https://www.irishmirror.ie/sport/ufc/social-media-expert-reveals-conor-13325944.

83. Kate Malczewski, "The Rock's Teremana Tequila tops 600,000 cases," The Spirits Business Blog, https://www.thespiritsbusiness.com/2021/12/the-rocks-teremana-tequila-tops-600000-cases/.

84. Gaurav Singh, "Dwayne Johnson's Earning From $3.5 Billion Worth Teremana Tequila: Who Are the Owners of the Rock's Tequila Brand?" Sports Manor Blog, https://www.sportsmanor.com/dwayne-johnson-earning-from-3-5-billion-worth-teremana-tequila-who-are-the-owners-of-the-rocks-tequila-brand/#:~:text=As%20per%20sources%2C%20the%20Teremana,the%20stake%20in%20the%20brand.

85. Christian Smith, "Conor McGregor sells majority of Proper No. Twelve to Proximo Spirits for reported $600m," The Drinks Business,

https://www.thedrinksbusiness.com/2021/04/conor-mcgregor-sells-majority-of-proper-no-twelve-to-proximo-spirits-for-reported-600m/.

86. Georgie Collins, "Teremana reaches one million case sales," The Spirits Business, https://www.thespiritsbusiness.com/2023/04/teremana-reaches-one-million-case-sales/.

87. Alex Hormozi, "Get Rich in the New Economy," Alex Hormozi's YouTube channel, https://www.youtube.com/watch?v=6DCDGSnRDtM.

88. Venturz, (2024), "50+ interesting sales funnel statistics," Venturz, https://venturz.co/blog/sales-funnel-statistics.

89. Camille Trent, (2022, February 7), "14 surprising sales funnel statistics to boost conversion rates in 2022," Dooly, https://www.dooly.ai/blog/sales-funnel-statistics/.

90. Chandraveer Singh, "100+ video marketing statistics: Surprising insights 2024" SocialPilot, https://www.socialpilot.co/blog/video-marketing-statistics.

91. Alban Brooke, (2024, September 11), "Podcast statistics and data [September 2024]," Buzzsprout. https://www.buzzsprout.com/blog/podcast-statistics.

NATE HAMBRICK

International Bestselling Author | High-Performance Strategist

Nate Hambrick has built a reputation as a relentless achiever and a master of leverage. He is best known for his books *Crush Your Kryptonite* and *The 18 Laws of Leverage*, which provide simple systems for building exponential wealth. Nate first transformed his financial future by building a diversified portfolio of 300+ passive income streams, including rental income, royalties, affiliate fees, and syndications.

Nate now devotes his time to teaching others how to use the laws of leverage to build lasting financial freedom for themselves and their families. Learn more at natehambrick.com